To that gentle owner of a huge
private joke, the good-natured
bringer of joy, beloved grandson,
MARK

# CONTENTS

# INTRODUCTION

There are few places in the world where some kind of machine or device is not working at this very moment. Looking around your own house, or just outside, you can probably count dozens of things right away. Refrigerators, automobiles, radios, television sets, toasters, doorbells, furnaces, and tape recorders are only a few.

How do these things work? What makes them do the things they do? They were all invented and built by human beings, so there is nothing mysterious about them. Nature may hold many secrets, but machines do not. We understand every machine and device we make. Some are extremely complicated, others only seem so, but it is possible to understand even the most complicated machine, once you are told how it works. This book describes a few of the things you can see working every day, and some—such as rockets—that you may not have a chance to see, but that you've heard a lot about.

If this book had been written for your grandparents, who were boys and girls only a short time ago in history, the things described would have been very different. Electrical devices, although in use, were not a part of almost everyone's life, as they are today. The only electronic device that might have been known by your grandfather or grandmother was a radio. Because electrical and electronic devices today play such a large part in our lives, much of this book has been devoted to them. For the same reason, the working of the automobile engine has been described in greater detail than the working of other engines.

Learning how something works is exciting and always fascinating. Furthermore, once you know how a machine or other device works, you will find the world around you a little different—a little friendlier.

# ELECTRICAL AND MAGNETIC DEVICES AND MACHINES

We are familiar with many electrical devices and machines because they are part of our daily lives. Many of them are in the home; we see or hear them working every day and we work some of them ourselves, such as the lights, the telephone, the toaster, the clock, the vacuum cleaner, etc. Motors run the refrigerator and air conditioner, pump on the oil heater, and fan on the hot-air heater. But to understand how these appliances work, we must first know something about electricity.

## ELECTRICITY

No one knows exactly what electricity is, but we do know a great deal about it—what it can do and how it works.

All matter is composed of extremely small particles called *atoms*. Our bodies are made up entirely of atoms, and so is the air we breathe and the water we drink. The paper these words are printed on and the ink they are printed with are both made up of atoms. A single atom is too tiny to be seen, even with the most powerful microscope. If you could place a hundred million average-sized atoms in a row, they would form a line just an inch long. Nearly 250 billion atoms could be placed in a single layer on the period at the end of this sentence.

1

Despite the smallness of atoms, scientists have learned much about them. An atom has a central part, the *nucleus*, around which other parts, called *electrons*, revolve in orbits in much the same way that planets revolve around the sun. There are differences, however. One is that each planet in our solar system revolves in its own orbit around the sun—but as many as 32 electrons revolve in a single orbit around a nucleus!

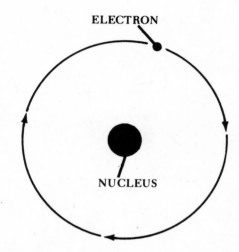

A second difference is that all the planets revolve in the same plane, but electrons do not. If you could put the sun through the center of a giant dinner plate, so that half the sun was above the plate and half below, the planets would lie on—or very nearly on—the surface of the plate. But if you could put the nucleus of an atom through a dinner plate, the orbits of only a few of the electrons would lie on the surface of the plate. Most of the orbits would curve over and under the plate in many different directions.

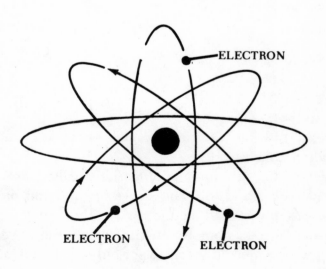

An atom, like the solar system, is mostly empty space. The nucleus and the electrons take up only one ten-thousandth of the total space occupied by the atom; therefore, you can see that an electron must be much smaller than an atom. No one knows the exact size of an electron, because no one, as yet, has been able to measure directly anything that small. But scientists know that an electron is smaller than one ten-million-millionth of an inch in diameter. The period at the end of this sentence could cover 250 thousand billion billion electrons in a single layer!

The nucleus is made up of two kinds of particles: *protons* and *neutrons*. Each of these protons and neutrons is about ten times as big as an electron. There are more than a hundred different kinds of atoms, and each one has a different number of electrons, protons, and neutrons. The exception is the smallest and lightest atom which has only one electron revolving around a nucleus made up of a single proton but no neutron. The largest atom has more than a hundred each of electrons, neutrons, and protons.

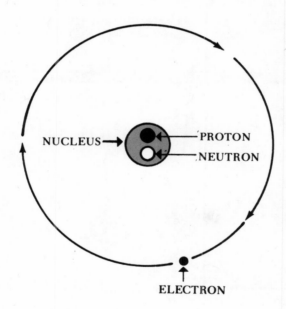

## Electric Charges

An electron is a unit—a single charge—of electricity. So is a proton. An electron is a charge of *negative* electricity. A negative electric charge is also called a *minus* charge, and is shown in writing by a minus sign: – . A proton is a charge of *positive* electricity. A positive charge is also called a *plus* charge and is shown in writing by a *plus* sign: + . A neutron has no electric charge; it is electrically *neutral*.

An electron and a proton very close together act as if they have no charges. We say that they *neutralize* each other. Any number of unit electric charges act the same way. A billion billion electrons in contact with a billion billion protons would form a group that is electrically neutral. Although the unit—that is, the smallest—electric charge is either a single electron or proton, an electric charge

3

may be made up of any number of either electrons or protons. A billion electrons, or 452,679 electrons, or three, or any number of electrons, each form a single charge of negative electricity. A million, or 180, or 560,779,226,408, or any number of protons, each form a single charge of positive electricity.

## Law of Electric Charges

There is one important fact to learn in order to understand how electric devices work. This fact is summed up in the Law of Electric Charges: *Like charges repel; unlike charges attract.* Two positive charges or two negative charges repel—push away—each other. But a negative and a positive charge attract—pull toward—each other.

Not all electrons are attached to atoms. Unattached electrons are called *free electrons* and play a very important part in electricity. An *electric current* is made up of a great many free electrons all moving in the same direction within a small space. An electric current in a wire is composed of vast numbers of free electrons all moving in the spaces between the atoms near the surface of the metal that makes up the wire.

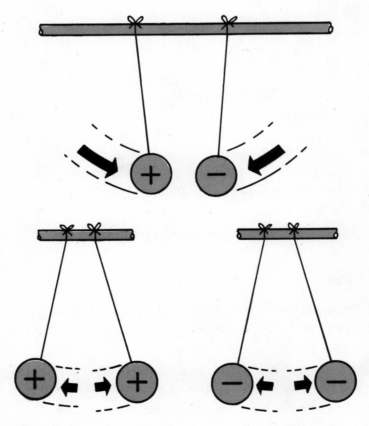

## Electrical Conductors

Materials through which electrons move easily are called *conductors*. Not all materials are equally good conductors. Good conductors are those which have large numbers of free electrons among their atoms, such as metals, which are the best conductors. The materials that have few free electrons conduct electricity so poorly that in most situations they actually block the flow of electric current. Materials through which electric current cannot flow under ordinary conditions are called *insulators*.

## Circuits

The path that electric current takes when it flows through any electrical machine or device is called a *circuit*. A circuit must be an unbroken path of material that conducts electric current. The path is endless, because the current travels around and around. For example, in a flashlight, there is a small electric light bulb lit by a storage battery. Electric current leaves one end of the battery and flows through a wire to the bulb. The current then passes through the bulb and returns to the battery through another wire. Entering the other end of the battery, the current moves through the battery, returning to where it began. The current has made a round trip and is about to start on another. The wire from the battery to the bulb, the brass base of the bulb, the wires in the bulb, the wire returning to the battery, and the materials inside the battery, all make up the circuit.

## Units of Electricity

Electric current flowing through a conductor, such as a wire, may be likened to water flowing through a hose. By placing a finger over the end of the hose, you can feel a force pressing against it. The more water entering the hose at the spigot, the greater will be the force of the water flowing through the hose. In much the same way, the more current (electrons) forced into a wire, the greater the force of the current in the wire. This current is called *electromotive force*, and the unit in which it is measured is the *volt*, named for Alessandro Volta (1745-1827), professor of physics at the University of Pavia, Italy, and one of the world's first great experimenters in electricity. Electromotive force is abbreviated *e.m.f.* and is also called *voltage*. A flashlight battery forces electrons along the wire in the flashlight bulb with an e.m.f. of 1 1/2 volts, so the voltage of the battery is 1 1/2.

To measure an amount of water that runs through a hose, you can measure the amount that flows past any point of the hose in a unit of time, say the amount of water flowing through the nozzle in one second. Similarly, to measure the electricity flowing through a wire, you measure the amount of current flowing past any point in the wire in one second. This amount of current is the unit of flow and is called an *ampere*. It is named for André Marie Ampére (1775-1836), a French physicist and mathematician. One ampere is equal to 6,281,000,000,000,000 electrons passing a point in a conductor in one second.

It is more difficult to send water through a hose having rough interior walls than through a hose having smooth walls. Rough walls hold back, or resist, the passage of the water. Electrons in the atoms of the wire resist the passage of electrons that make up a current. The unit in which resistance is measured is the *ohm*. It is named for Georg Simon Ohm (1787-1854), a German physicist. If an e.m.f. of one volt is needed to push a current of one ampere through a conductor, then the conductor has a resistance of one ohm.

To remember the units used for measuring electric current, refer to this table:

| What is measured | Electrical term | Unit of Measurement |
|---|---|---|
| force of current | voltage, e.m.f. | volt |
| amount of current | amperage | ampere |
| resistance to current | resistance | ohm |

## MAGNETISM

Magnetism and electricity are so closely connected and depend so much on each other that to understand electricity and how electric things work, you must learn how magnets and magnetism work. A magnet is a piece of metal that can attract iron readily, and nickel and cobalt to a lesser degree. A magnet attracts certain metal alloys very strongly. The invisible force that enables a magnet to attract these metals is called *magnetism*. As with electricity, no one knows exactly what magnetism is, but scientists do know a lot about what it does.

If a magnet is suspended by its middle on a string, so that it can swing freely, the magnet will come to rest with one end pointing toward, but not exactly at, the North Pole. The other end will be pointing, of course, toward the South Pole. The end that points toward the North Pole is called the *north pole* of the magnet. The other end is the magnet's *south pole*.

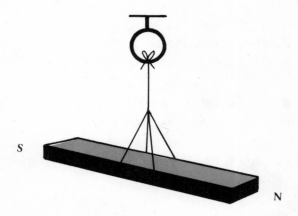

The space around a magnet in which its magnetism—that is, its lines of magnet force—can be detected is called the *field* of the magnet.

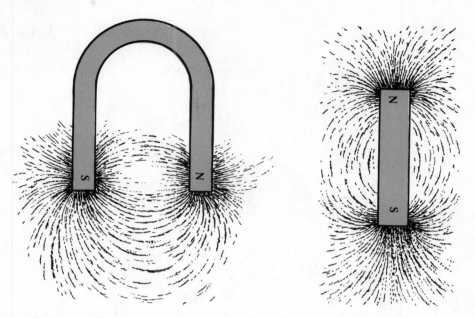

If you were to break a bar magnet in two, you would probably expect to find that one half of it possesses the north pole and the other half the south pole. Yet if you were to test the two halves, you would again find two complete magnets, each with a north and a south pole. Even if you were to break the halves into quarters, and the quarters into eighths, and so on, until you had very small pieces, you would find that each piece is a complete magnet with both a north and a south pole. This phenomenon led the German scientist, Wilhelm Weber, to surmise, a century ago, that each individual atom of a piece of magnetic material is itself a magnet, with a north and south pole of its own.

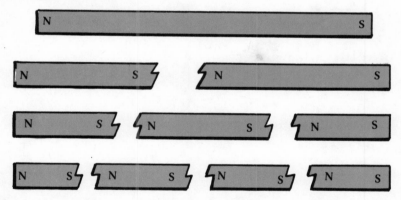

Weber's theory was correct. Physicists have since learned that as an electron revolves around the nucleus of an atom, the electron spins on its axis. Because of this spin, the electron generates a magnetic field. Thus, an electron is the smallest known magnet.

The magnetic properties of certain materials are the result of the way the magnetic fields of the atoms are lined up. Magnetic materials have groups of atoms whose magnetic fields are more or less permanently lined up. These groups of atoms are called *magnetic domains*. In an unmagnetized piece of material that is capable of being magnetized, the domains are arranged in a haphazard manner. As the material becomes more magnetized, additional magnetic domains line up with their north poles all pointing in one direction and their south poles in the opposite direction. When the majority of the domains have been lined up, a material is magnetized; it has become a magnet.

**NOT MAGNETIZED**

**PARTIALLY MAGNETIZED**

**MAGNETIZED**

## Law of Magnetic Poles

A very important fact about magnets is contained in the Law of Magnetic Poles: *Like poles repel; unlike poles attract.* Two north poles or two south poles placed close together will repel—push away—each other. A north pole and a south pole will attract—pull toward—each other.

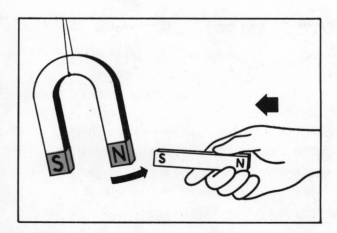 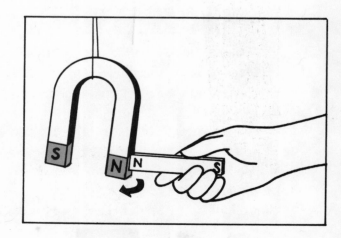

You can easily see the similarity between the Law of Magentic Poles and the Law of Electric Charges. It would lead you to believe that there is a close relationship between electricity and magnetism. Scientists agree, but they have not yet been able to find out exactly what that relationship is.

## Electromagnet

You may have seen a crane in a junkyard lower a thick metal disc into a pile of scrap metal. When the crane raised the disc, the body of an automobile and several large and small pieces of metal were attached to it, though no ropes or chains held these things to the disc. Then the crane moved the disc and its burden to another part of the junkyard, and the automobile body and the pieces of iron fell upon a junk pile beneath the disc. Within the disc were one or more *electromagnets*.

When an electric current flows through a conductor, such as a wire, the current

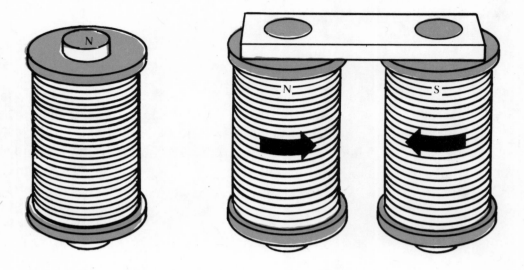

produces a magnetic field around the conductor. This fact is used in making an electromagnet. The device consists of a bar of magnetic material, such as soft iron, around and around which a wire is wound (above, left). The bar is called the *core* of the magnet; the turns of wire make up the *coil*. The reason the core is made of soft iron is that this metal is easily magnetized and just as easily demagnetized. There are several alloys that share this property with soft iron and are used in making cores for electromagnets.

When an electric current is sent through the coil, the lines of magnetic force produced by the current are concentrated in the core. When the current is cut off, the core loses practically all of its magnetism immediately. This is how the electromagnet used in the junkyard could be made to pick up and then drop its burden of scrap metal.

Although some electromagnets consist of a single core and coil, in practice an electromagnet usually consists of two cores and coils. The cores are joined at one end by a metal bar. The two coils are wound in opposite directions. As a result, the free end of one core is a north magnetic pole and the other is a south magnetic pole (above, right).

The strength of an electromagnet depends mainly on three things: the number of turns of wire in the coil, the strength of the current flowing through the coil, and the kind of metal used for the core. More turns of wire result in a stronger magnetic field. Increasing the number of turns, however, increases resistance to current. Therefore, there is a limit to the number of turns of wire that can be used efficiently. Also, a stronger current results in a stronger magnet. But here, too, there is a limit; too strong a current will heat the coils, burning them out. Certain iron alloys make cores that are more strongly magnetic than others.

## Electric Generator, or Dynamo

If you move a conductor through a magnetic field, an electric current will be produced in the conductor. For example, if you move a coil of wire between the north and south poles of a magnet, you will produce an electric current in the wire of the coil. This is what is accomplished in an electric generator, or *dynamo*. The coil is called the *armature*, and the magnet is called a *field magnet*.

There are small electric generators, called *magnetos*, in which a coil of wire is rapidly rotated on an axle between the poles of a permanent magnet. (A permanent magnet is one made from a metallic alloy that, unlike soft iron, does not lose its magnetism when a magnetizing force is taken away.) The current generated in the armature must be conducted away. Wires cannot simply be connected to the armature, because the turning armature would quickly wrap the wires around the axle. To solve this problem, flat metal rings, called *slip rings*, are attached to the axle. (*See illustration, top of following page.*) Two straight, flat pieces of metal, called *brushes,* are arranged so that they brush against the slip rings. Wires are attached to the brushes to take the generated electric current to where it is to be used. Magnetos are used to provide electric current for the spark plugs of outboard motors, motorcycles, lawnmowers and other machines with small engines.

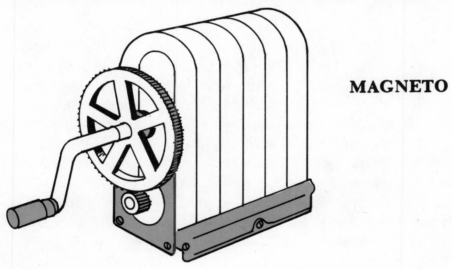

**MAGNETO**

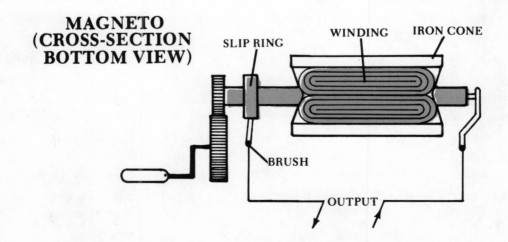

**MAGNETO (CROSS-SECTION BOTTOM VIEW)**

SLIP RING  WINDING  IRON CONE

BRUSH

OUTPUT

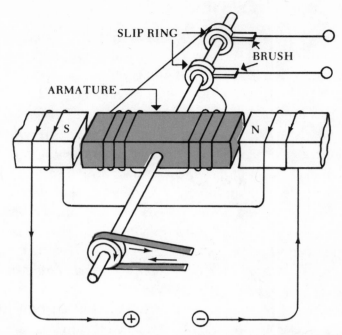

SLIP RING

BRUSH

ARMATURE

S

N

## ALTERNATING-CURRENT GENERATOR

In larger generators, the field magnet is an electromagnet and the coil is made of thousands of turns of insulated wire. The current for the electromagnet may come from a storage battery or it may be taken from the current produced by the generator itself. The armature may be turned by a gasoline or diesel engine or by an electric motor that gets its current from a source other than the generator. The arrangement of slip rings and branches is the same as in a magneto.

If you reverse the direction in which a conductor is moving through a magnetic field, you reverse the direction in which the produced current flows. When an armature spins between the poles of a field magnet, the wires of the coil move through the magnetic field first in one direction and then in the opposite direction during each turn of the armature. This makes the generated current flow first in one direction and then in the opposite direction. Such a current is called *alternating current*, and is abbreviated *a.c.* This is the kind of current that is used to light bulbs and run refrigerators, vacuum cleaners and other electric appliances in most cities and towns.

For many purposes, such as charging storage batteries, refining metals from ores, and plating metals, alternating current cannot be used. What is needed is current that flows in one direction only. This can be produced by a *direct current* (*d.c.*) generator. To obtain direct current from a generator, an ingenious device called a *commutator,* or reversing switch, is used. (*See illustration, top of following page.*) A commutator is simply a split flat ring. Each half of the split ring is attached to a different end of the armature coil. The brushes are arranged so that each brush is connected first with one end of the armature coil and then with the

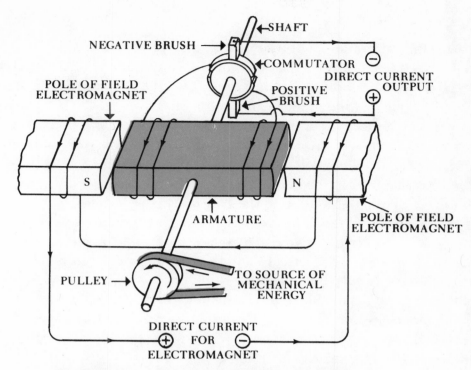

**DIRECT-CURRENT GENERATOR**

other end as the armature revolves. As a result, just at the moment that the current would reverse itself, the split in the ring reaches the brush and the other half of the ring feeds current to the brush. Thus, the current never reverses direction.

Split rings and brushes are troublesome; they burn out and wear out. To do away with brushes and split rings on alternating-current generators, the armature is made up of many coils arranged in a ring and is stationary. Such an armature is called a *stator*. The electromagnet, called a *rotor*, turns within the stator. Since the current is generated in the coils of the stator, which does not move, the current can be led away from the generator without the problems caused by a spinning armature. The stator-rotor arrangement is found in the generators of electric generating plants in cities and towns. The generators in these plants have stators 25 feet in diameter, containing tens of thousands of turns of wire in their coils. The huge rotors that fit into these stators are turned by steam turbines or by turbines powered by water falling through a dam.

In any kind of device that produces electricity, the part **from** which the negative charges (electrons) flow is called the *negative pole*, or *cathode*. The part **to** which the negative charges flow is called the *positive pole*, or *anode*. Either an anode *or* a cathode may be also called an *electrode*. The end of an anode or a cathode that is connected to an electric circuit is called a *terminal*.

The following table will help you remember the terms connected with positive and negative electricity:

| negative | minus | (=) | electron | cathode | "from" |
|----------|-------|-----|----------|---------|--------|
| positive | plus  | (+) | proton   | anode   | "to"   |

## Electric Motor

Turning an armature between the poles of an electromagnet (field magnet) generates electric current that flows *out* of the armature. What would happen if we reversed the situation and sent current *into* the armature? The armature would turn. This fact is used to make an electric motor.

By sending electric current into an armature, we make an electromagnet of the armature. Then we have one magnet, the armature, within another, the field magnet. The field magnet may be either a permanent magnet or an electromagnet. Each magnet has its own north and south magnetic poles. The poles will act toward each other according to the Law of Magnetic Poles.

When current enters the wires of the coil, the armature becomes an electromagnet. The like poles (the two north poles and two south poles) of the armature and the field magnet repel each other; the unlike poles (one north and one south) attract. As a result, the armature turns untils the north and south poles have moved as close as possible to each other. When this has happened, the attraction of the unlike poles should prevent the armature from turning any farther.

Just before the unlike magnetic poles face each other, the commutator on the armature axle reverses the direction of the current. With current flowing into the armature from the opposite direction, the poles of the armature are reversed; the north pole becomes a south pole and the south pole becomes a north pole. Now, the poles of the armature and field magnet that face each other are like poles. The like poles repel, and the armature makes another half-turn.

As rapidly as the armature spins, the commutator reverses the direction of the incoming current, the magnetic poles continually reverse, and the armature continues to turn. Some armatures turn more than a thousand times a minute.

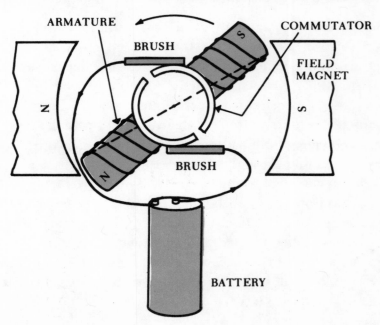

An electric motor is one of the most useful machines we have. Push a button or snap a switch, and an electric motor works immediately, powerfully and quietly. Think how clumsy it would be to run an electric fan or kitchen mixer with a gasoline or steam engine! Electric motors run refrigerators, air conditioners, drills, typewriters, shavers, washing machines and scores of other useful appliances.

Powerful electric motors have many uses in industry. They run elevators and hoists that lift heavy loads. They move conveyor belts of assembly lines. They run subways, streetcars, and trains.

## Doorbell

A doorbell uses an electromagnet. The button outside the door is a switch. When the button is pushed, electric current flows into the coiled wire of the electromagnet that is part of the bell. The magnet attracts and pulls on a magnetic metal strip, the armature. At the top of the strip is a knob, or clapper, that strikes the bell. *(See illustration below.)*

Once you have pushed the button, closing the circuit and pulling the armature toward the electromagnet, you might think that the armature would remain in contact with the magnet until you release the button. But, of course, this is not what happens. Instead, as long as the finger is held on the button, the armature

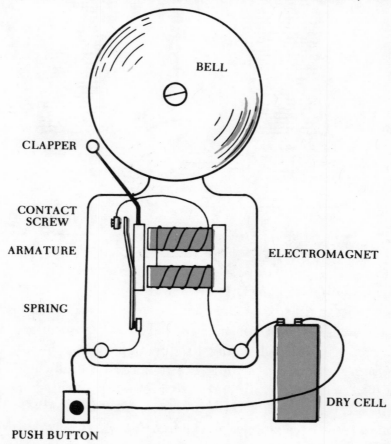

leaps rapidly back and forth, banging the clapper on the bell. This happens because the armature is attached to a springy strip of brass that is in contact with a pointed screw, called the *contact screw*. Electric current, after passing through the brass strip, enters the electromagnet by way of the contact screw. As soon as the electromagnet pulls the armature, the attached brass strip is also pulled toward the magnet and away from the contact screw, breaking the circuit. When this happens there is no electric current in the circuit, and the electromagnet cannot work; it no longer pulls on the armature. The brass strip springs back, pulling the armature with it, and touches the contact screw again. The circuit is reestablished, and the whole sequence of events repeats itself.

A buzzer works the same way a bell does, but it makes a buzzing sound because the clapper strikes a solid object instead of a hollow bell.

The bell and buzzer we have just described are powered by dry cell batteries which produce direct current (d.c.). Some doorbells, and almost all telephone bells, are powered by alternating current (a.c.). These work differently from battery-powered bells.

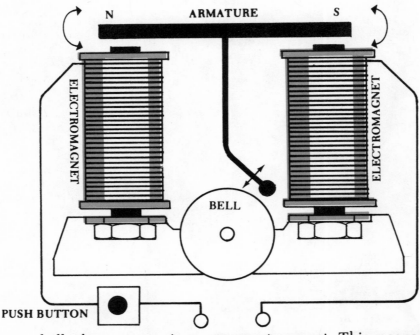

In an a.c. bell, the armature is a permanent magnet. This means that its north and south poles do not change. The armature is arranged so that it can swing on a pivot through its middle. *(See illustration above.)* It is located just above the poles of an electromagnet. Alternating current flowing through the coils of the electromagnet is rapidly changing its direction. The poles of the magnet keep changing from north to south and south to north as rapidly as the current changes direction. The poles of the armature are alternately repelled and attracted by the poles of the electromagnet, and the armature tilts back and forth. Attached to the armature is a rod with a clapper on the free end. As the armature swings back and forth, the knob strikes a bell.

16

## Kilowatt-Hour Meter

You have probably read the words printed on the tops of light bulbs. In addition to the name of the bulb's manufacturer and the number of volts needed to operate the bulb properly, there is printed "25 watts," "50 watts" or some other number of watts. What does "watt" mean?

Energy is the ability to do work. Electricity, in many kinds of machines, does a lot of work. Therefore, electricity is a form of energy—electrical energy. Electric power is the amount of work done by electrical energy in a specific unit of time, such as a second. The most common unit in which electric power is measured is the *watt*, named for James Watt (1736-1819), a Scottish inventor who perfected the first practical steam engine. One watt is the amount of power that would raise an object weighing approximately 1 1/3 pounds to a height of one foot in one second.

The electrical power used in houses and office and factory buildings is measured in *kilowatt-hours*. "Kilo" means thousand, so a kilowatt is one thousand watts. One kilowatt-hour is one thousand watts of power used continuously for one hour. If a 200-watt electric light bulb is lit continuously for five hours, it uses 1000 (200 x 5) watt-hours, or one kilowatt-hour of power.

An electric company charges its customers for electric power measured in kilowatt-hours. The power used by the consumer is measured by a watt-hour meter, a measuring device usually placed where the main wires enter the building. The meter is a small electric motor whose speed is proportionate to the power used. The armature of the motor is a thin disc, which is affixed to a shaft; and the shaft is connected by gears and other shafts to the pointers of register dials.

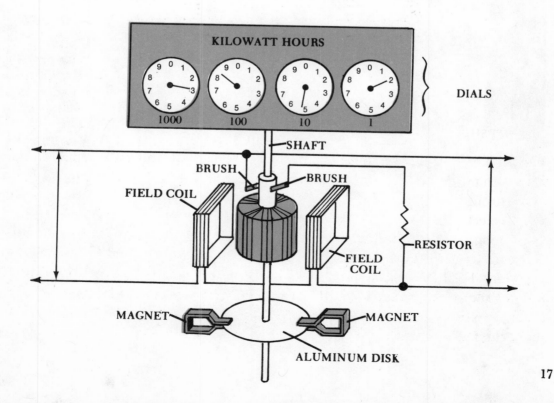

17

Each dial is numbered from 1 to 9, and the sizes of the gears are arranged so that one complete turn of the pointer on one dial—from 0 around to 0—moves the pointer on the next dial at the left just one number, say from 2 to 3. Notice that each dial is numbered in the opposite direction from the one next to it.

The sizes of the gear are arranged so that the dial at the right registers in kilowatt-hours. The next dial registers in units of ten kilowatt-hours; the next in hundred kilowatt-hours; and the dial at the left in thousand kilowatt-hours.

## Telephone

In a telephone, sound is changed into electric current and electric current is changed into sound.

Sound is made when the particles that make up a gas (such as air), a liquid (such as water), or a solid (such as iron or wood) move rapidly back and forth. This back-and-forth motion is called *vibration*. When an object vibrates in air, the object pushes air outward from itself in a series of air-waves. When these waves strike our ears, we hear a sound. For example, when a gong is struck, the gong vibrates. The metal shell of the gong moves first in one direction, then in the opposite direction. When any portion of the shell moves in one direction, it squeezes together air particles in its path as it shoves them outward. As the same portion of the shell moves in the opposite direction, the air particles behind it are spaced out. (Of course, when the air on one side of the vibrating portion is being squeezed together, the air on the other side is being spaced out.) The alternate squeezing and thinning out of air particles produces sound waves.

The telephone has two main parts. One is the part you speak into, the *transmitter;* the other is the part you listen to, the *receiver.*

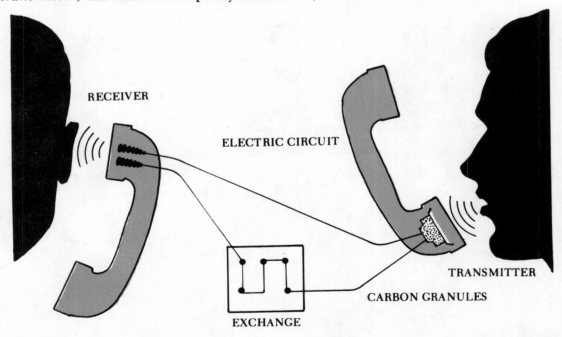

RECEIVER

ELECTRIC CIRCUIT

TRANSMITTER

CARBON GRANULES

EXCHANGE

As with all apparatus using electric current, the telephone must have a complete electric circuit in order to work. When you dial a number, an automatic switch in the telephone exchange completes a circuit between your telephone and the telephone of the person you are calling. The electric current is supplied by generators at the telephone company.

A small, round, flat box filled with grains of carbon is contained inside the transmitter. The top of this box is a thin metal disc, called a diaphragm. As you talk into the phone, the sound waves of your voice cause the diaphragm to vibrate. The back-and-forth movement of the diaphragm alternately squeezes the carbon grains together and then leaves them room to spread out.

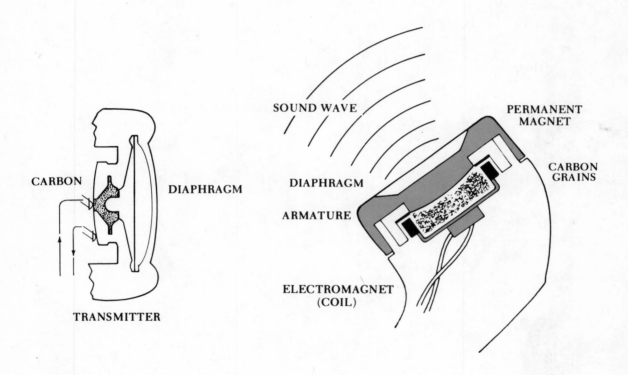

The carbon grains are part of an electric circuit, and current can pass through them more easily when they are packed tightly together than when they are spread out. For this reason, the amount of current that flows through the carbon grains varies from moment to moment as the diaphragm vibrates.

The changing current flows along a wire to the telephone exchange and then to the receiver of the phone being used by the person to whom you are talking. Inside the receiver is a ring-shaped permanent magnet, the armature, and inside the ring is a coil of very fine wire. When electric current flows into the coil, the ring-shaped magnet becomes an electromagnet. In front of the electromagnet is a thin, springy, iron disc, the receiver diaphragm.

As electric current from the telephone wire enters the coil with varying strength, the strength of the electromagnet also varies proportionately. When the electromagnetic field is strong, the diaphragm bows inward toward the coil. (*See illustration below.*) When the field is weak, the diaphragm springs back, bowing outward. The particles of air in contact with the diaphragm are alternately squeezed together and thinned out, as the diaphragm moves back and forth. The vibrating diaphragm produces sound waves. Sound waves activated by the diaphragm of the receiver are the same kind as those made by sounds spoken into the transmitter.

The important thing to understand about how a telephone works is that it is not sound itself that travels along the wires. It is electric current of continually changing strength, the changes in strength being produced by the transmitter and changed to sound by the receiver.

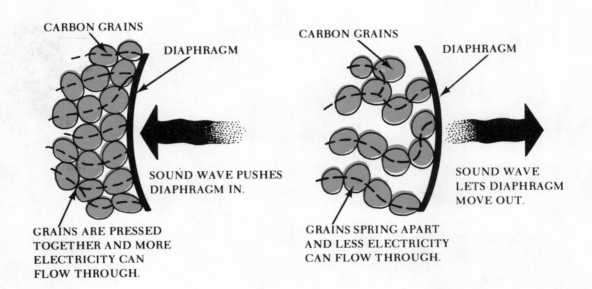

CARBON GRAINS

DIAPHRAGM

SOUND WAVE PUSHES DIAPHRAGM IN.

GRAINS ARE PRESSED TOGETHER AND MORE ELECTRICITY CAN FLOW THROUGH.

CARBON GRAINS

DIAPHRAGM

SOUND WAVE LETS DIAPHRAGM MOVE OUT.

GRAINS SPRING APART AND LESS ELECTRICITY CAN FLOW THROUGH.

## Transformer

A transformer is a device used with *alternating current* to change low voltage to high, or high to low. There are many types of transformers, but all have certain basic features in common. Two coils of insulated wire are wound on opposite sides of an iron core that has the shape of a square letter "o." The core usually is laminated, which means that it is made up of several layers fastened together. The two coils are not connected to each other. The coil through which current enters the transformer is called the *primary*; the coil through which the current leaves the transformer is the *secondary*. If the secondary coil has more turns of wire than the primary, the current leaving the transformer will have a higher voltage than the entering current. This kind of transformer is called a *step-up* transformer. If the

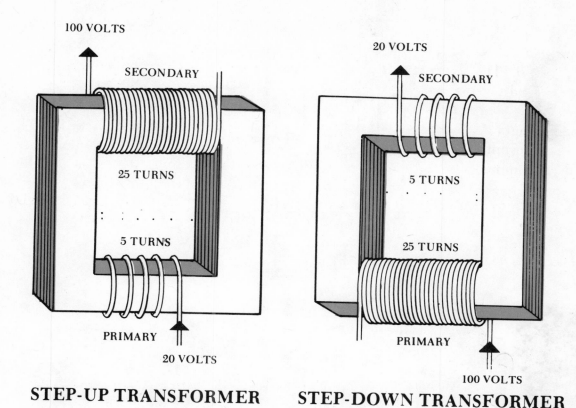

100 VOLTS

SECONDARY

25 TURNS

5 TURNS

PRIMARY

20 VOLTS

20 VOLTS

SECONDARY

5 TURNS

25 TURNS

PRIMARY

100 VOLTS

**STEP-UP TRANSFORMER**     **STEP-DOWN TRANSFORMER**

secondary coil has fewer turns of wire than the primary, the current leaving the transformer will have a lower voltage than the entering current. This type of transformer is called a *step-down* transformer.

All wires, even those made of metals that are very good conductors of electricity, offer resistance to the flow of electric current. From this fact you can easily see that the longer a wire is, the greater its total resistance will be to current passing through it.

The a.c. electric current used in most houses has a voltage—an electromotive force—of 110 to 120. But if the current had left the electric-power generating plant with an e.m.f. of 110 to 120 volts by the time it had flowed on its way to distant houses, the voltage would have been so low that it would have been very difficult, if not impossible, to detect it. The resistance of miles of wire would have lowered the voltage. Thus, to make sure that current will be effective at long distances, it is sent out of the power plant at 220,000 volts or more. This high voltage has enough electromotive force to push through the resistance of miles of wire.

The power plant generates alternating current at 2,200 volts, and step-up transformers raise the voltage to 220,000.

When the electric current nears the city or town in which it is to be used, step-down transformers lower the e.m.f. to 2,200 volts. Then, upon entering a neighborhood or housing development, the voltage is lowered again, this time to

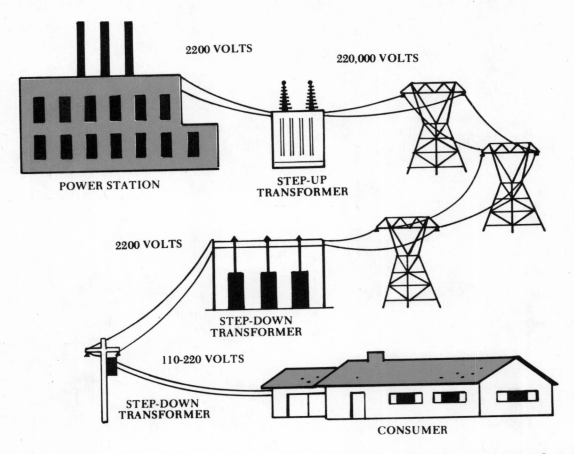

2200 VOLTS

220,000 VOLTS

POWER STATION

STEP-UP
TRANSFORMER

2200 VOLTS

STEP-DOWN
TRANSFORMER

110-220 VOLTS

STEP-DOWN
TRANSFORMER

CONSUMER

220. Finally, current entering houses is stepped down to between 120 and 110 volts. Near your house, you may see one of the final step-down transformers—a large, round black box atop a utility pole.

## Tape Recorder

A tape recorder is an electrical device that records sound on a special kind of tape. The sounds can be played back whenever you wish. You can keep for as long as you want a speech, an interview, a musical performance, a radio broadcast, the sound portion of a television broadcast, a baby's first words, or any other sound recorded on the tape.

A tape recorder uses a microphone that works much like a telephone transmitter, changing sound waves to impulses of electric current of varying strength. An important difference is that sound entering the microphone generates the current. From the microphone, the electrical impulses, which are weak, go through a wire to an electronic device that strengthens, or amplifies, them. From the amplifier, the current goes to a *recording head*, which is an electromagnet. The magnet's iron core is in the shape of a ring, and the coil is inside the ring. *(See illustration, top of following page.)* The magnetic field produced by the recording head varies from strong to weak, depending on the strength of the current from the microphone.

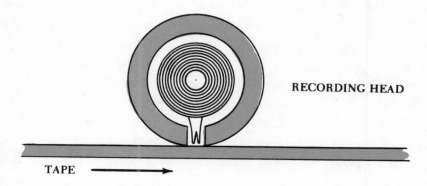

RECORDING HEAD

TAPE ⟶

The tape is made of two layers of plastic ribbon. Sandwiched between the layers is powdered iron oxide, a substance that is very easily magnetized and demagnetized. There are two types of recorders, depending on how the tape is handled. A *reel* recorder has two large reels: one is called the *storage reel* and the other is the *take-up reel*. A *cassette* recorder also has storage and take-up reels, but they are much smaller, and both reels are sealed in a small plastic box, which is the cassette. The reel from which the tape is unwinding is the storage reel; the reel upon which the tape is being wound is the take-up reel. Each reel fits on an axle, or *drive*, which is turned by an electric motor. Separate switches start and stop each drive. The drives turn in either direction, so that the tape may be wound on either reel. Only one drive turns at a time—the one turning the reel on which the tape is winding.

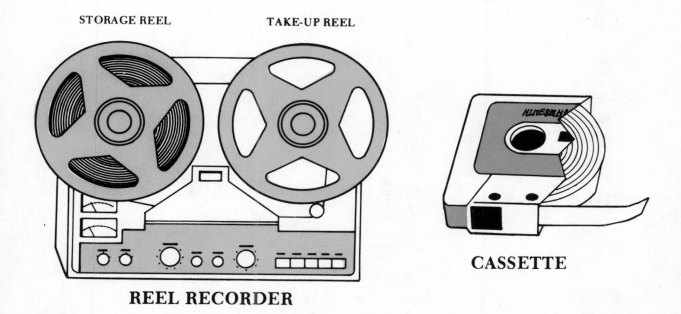

STORAGE REEL          TAKE-UP REEL

**REEL RECORDER**

**CASSETTE**

When you start to record with a reel recorder, all the tape will be on the storage reel. The beginning of the tape is threaded through a slit between the recording head and a small metal spool that turns freely on an axle. Then the tape is threaded around a device called a *capstan*. This is a small metal spindle on an axle that is held in position by a spring. The capstan puts slight tension on the tape because of the action of the spring, keeping it from running slack and helping it to wind neatly on the take-up reel. From the capstan the tape is taken to the take-up reel where it is threaded into a slit in the hub of the reel, or it may be attached to the hub by some other device.

When starting to record with a cassette recorder, the cassette is simply dropped into a compartment. The reels fit over the drives, and the spindle of the capstan goes through a hole in the bottom of the cassette.

When the motor is turned on, the take-up reel begins to turn, winding the tape around its hub. The tape unwinding from the storage reel passes between the recording head and the small metal spool. There is a notch in the iron ring of the recording head at the point where it meets the spool. The variations in the magnetic field produced by the recording head magnetize the tape as it moves past the notch. The tape, magnetized to varying strengths all along its length, winds on the take-up reel.

To play the tape recorder—that is, to cause the tape to reproduce the sound that was recorded—you must first rewind the tape on the storage reel. A switch and gears within the recorder turn the rewinding storage reel much faster than the recording take-up reel turned. A recording that took one hour to wind on the take-up reel is rewound in less than two minutes. When all the tape is rewound on the reel, the rewind switch is turned off. The tape is now sent in the opposite direction, winding on the take-up reel again at exactly the same speed as when the recording was made. Now, however, the magnetized tape passes over a device called a *playback head*. The magnetism in the tape produces electric currents of varying strength in a circuit that includes a loudspeaker. The sound-producing part of the speaker is much like a telephone receiver; the variations in current strength cause an electromagnet to vibrate a diaphragm that makes sound waves exactly like those that entered the microphone.

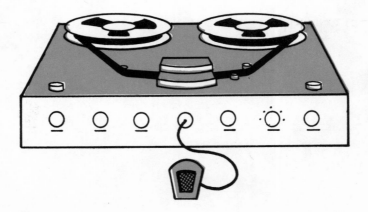

Portable recorders use dry cell electric batteries, and large complex recorders, such as those used in studios to record professional musicians and singers, operate on current obtained from wall sockets.

Recording tape is one-fourth of an inch wide. Usually, sound is recorded on only half of the tape's width at a time. Some recorders, however, put four recordings on a single width of tape. Reels of tapes are made in standard lengths that run for either half an hour or an hour. By putting the usual two tracks on a tape, you can obtain one to two hours of recording. A recording can be stopped at any time, rewound, and played back. Several recordings can be put on one tape.

Sound can be erased from recording tape by running the tape through an erasing head when a circuit in the recorder sends alternating current. This current jumbles up the magnetic alignment of atoms in the iron oxide, and the tape is once again ready to accept a new recording.

ALIGNED                                    ERASING HEAD
IRON

It is not necessary, however, to first erase sound from a tape if you want to make a new recording on it. You can simply record over the recording that is already on the tape. The magnetic impulses produced by the new sounds and the electromagnet will rearrange the magnetic alignment of the tape, automatically erasing the old recording.

A magnetic tape can be played over and over again without harming the quality of the recording. By comparison, the recording on a phonograph disc becomes poorer every time it is played, since the needle is gradually wearing down the grooves on the surface.

## ELECTRIC CELLS AND BATTERIES

The use of a coil and field magnet, as in an electric generator, is not the only means of producing electric current. Another very common way of producing electric current is by chemical means. Certain devices can change chemical energy to electrical energy. These devices are *electric cells*.

Many people mistakenly call an electric cell an electric "battery"; for instance, you may talk about a flashlight "battery." The term is not correct. A battery is a group of two or more cells being used together. So, you should speak of flashlight "cells," or the "battery" of a flashlight, if the flashlight uses two or more cells.

## Wet Cell

A *wet cell*, or *voltaic cell*, is an electric cell in which chemicals dissolved in water produce the electric current. Let us see how a very simple wet cell works. This cell consists of a watertight container, which might be a small glass bowl or a wide-mouthed glass jar. The container is filled about three-quarters full with a solution of the chemical, ammonium chloride, dissolved in water. The chemical solution in a wet cell is called an *electrolyte*. A carbon rod is placed on one side of the container in the electrolyte, and a zinc rod is placed in the other side.

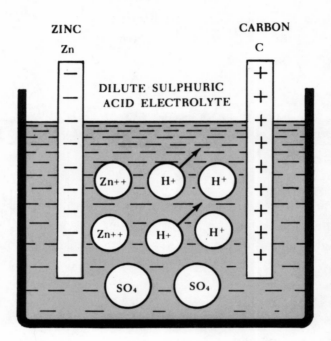

The zinc rod begins to dissolve in the solution. In this process, each zinc atom leaves behind one electron on the zinc rod. These electrons repel each other because they are all negative electric charges—and, as we already know, like charges repel each other. These electrons repel the free electrons in the upper part of the zinc rod. Meanwhile, the carbon rod is losing electrons to the electrolyte. For each electron lost, a positive charge is left behind on the carbon rod, which becomes a charged positive. The positive charges repel each other and push upward in the rod. After a very short time, the zinc rod has so strong a negative charge that it prevents any more zinc atoms from dissolving; and the carbon rod becomes so strongly charged positive that it can no longer lose electrons to the electrolyte. When this happens, the chemical action in the cell stops.

Now, if the zinc rod is connected to the carbon rod by a wire, the electrons have somewhere to go. They are repelled onto the wire. As they move, they repel toward the carbon rod the free electrons in the wire. Meanwhile, the free electrons in the part of the wire near the carbon rod are attracted to the positive charges on the rod. A movement of electrons thus takes place all along the wire, creating the electric current produced by the cell.

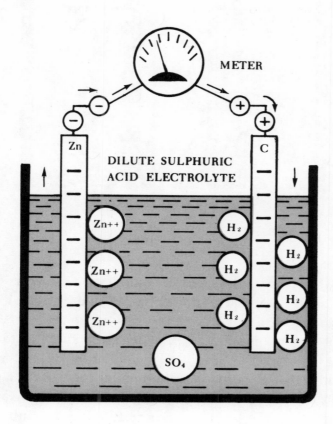

Instead of simply letting the current flow from the zinc cathode to the carbon anode, the current can be made to do work by connecting the cathode and anode to some kind of electrical device, perhaps a small current-measuring meter.

The cell will continue to produce electricity for some time because chemical reactions within the solution continue to provide the zinc with extra electrons and to take up electrons from the carbon. Eventually, the cell stops producing electricity. Bubbles of hydrogen gas, which come from one of the many chemical reactions taking place in the solution, cover the carbon anode and prevent any more electrons from leaving. This ends the flow of electrons, and the current stops.

When a cell can no longer produce a current because bubbles coat the anode, the cell is said to be *polarized*.

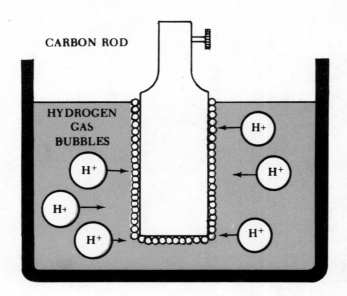

CARBON ROD

HYDROGEN
GAS
BUBBLES

## Storage Battery

One of the most successful wet cells to come out of 175 years of experimenting with various materials as anodes and cathodes and various materials as electrolytes, is the type used in a storage battery. You probably are familiar with the storage battery of an automobile that provides electricity for starting the engine, for the spark plugs, and for the lights, radio, and cigarette lighter.

The kind of storage battery used in an automobile consists of a group of three or six wet cells. The anode and cathode are grids made of an alloy of lead and antimony. The spaces in the positive grid are filled with a substance called lead peroxide, while spaces in the negative grid are filled with spongy lead. The electrolyte is a solution of sulfuric acid in water. Cells are connected so that the battery can provide electric current from all cells at the same time.

As electric current flows out of the battery, both the lead peroxide and the spongy lead change to a substance called lead sulfate. The electrolyte becomes a much weaker solution of sulfuric acid. As these changes take place, the cells give off less and less current, and we say that the battery is *discharging*, or running down.

After a storage battery has become discharged, it can be made to produce electricity again by sending direct current (d.c.) from some outside source through the battery. The current changes the lead sulfate back to spongy lead and lead peroxide, and the weak sulfuric acid solution becomes stronger. Each cell of the battery becomes almost the same as it was before the battery began to discharge.

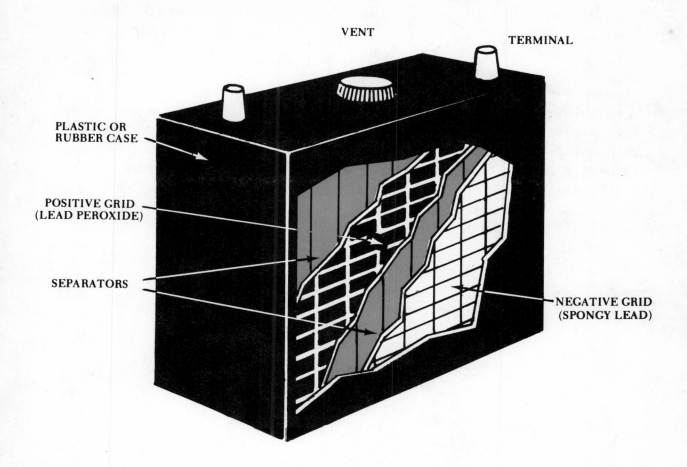

VENT

TERMINAL

PLASTIC OR
RUBBER CASE

POSITIVE GRID
(LEAD PEROXIDE)

SEPARATORS

NEGATIVE GRID
(SPONGY LEAD)

The process of bringing a discharged storage battery back to its original strength is called *charging*. But there is a limit to the number of times a storage battery can be charged. Chemical changes within the cells eventually make it impossible to bring the battery back to its original strength. When used in an automobile and given proper care, a lead-acid storage battery will last between three and four years.

If you think about the process of charging, you will understand how the storage battery got its name. Electric current is sent into the battery; then electric current comes out. It seems as though the battery had *stored* the electricity sent into it during charging. What really happened was that the current sent into the cells caused chemical changes that produced substances needed to make a wet cell ready to generate electric current.

The cells of a storage battery are almost completely enclosed in a plastic or hard rubber case. This is done so that the electrolyte, which is an acid, will not spill when the battery is moved about, as when an automobile goes around a curve, or starts or stops suddenly. The enclosure of the battery is not complete because there are small holes in the top of the case to allow the escape of gas which forms during the chemical reactions that take place when the battery is producing current. At best, a lead-acid storage battery is unwieldy and heavy. It must be kept

29

in a fairly upright position to prevent the electrolyte from spilling, and it must be ventilated to allow for the escape of gas. An automobile battery may weigh from slightly less than thirty to more than sixty pounds. The unwieldiness and weight are not disadvantages when the battery is used in an automobile, but a lead-acid battery is impractical for powering portable electric devices.

There are other storage batteries besides the lead-acid kind. Several are more efficient, but they are also more expensive. In the better ones, the metals used for the anodes and cathodes are nickel and iron, copper and zinc, or silver and zinc. One of the best is the nickel-cadmium battery, which has steel grids, the cathode grid containing cadmium and iron oxides, and the anode grid containing nickel hydroxide and graphite. The electrolyte is a solution of potassium hydroxide in water. And the complete battery is enclosed in a steel case.

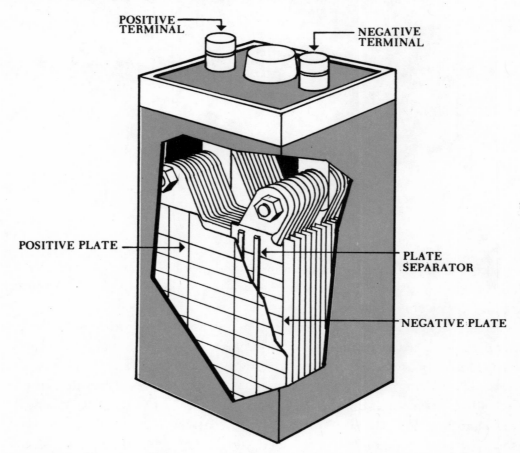

A nickel-cadmium battery weighs less than a lead-acid battery that produces an equal amount of current. Unlike a lead cell, a nickel-cadmium cell can be entirely sealed, eliminating the possibility of spilling the electrolyte, as well as the need for ventilation. This fact has resulted in the development of small nickel-cadmium batteries to provide power for flashlights, photographic flashguns, portable radios and television sets, and portable tools, such as electric drills. Like other storage batteries, a nickel-cadmium battery can be charged when it has run down. It can last as long as twenty years, far longer than any other wet-cell battery.

## Dry Cell

Fortunately, the world did not have to wait for the development of small nickel-cadmium batteries to power portable electric devices. A fine source of electricity that made them operate was the *dry cell*. You have seen dry cells in flashlights, portable radios, and flash cameras. Dry cells are quite efficient. The small rectangular ones that provide current for transistor radios generate an e.m.f. of 9 volts, which is more than the e.m.f. of some automobile storage batteries. (The dry cells provide much less total current, however, than the auto batteries.) Some dry cells used in scientific earth satellites are smaller than an aspirin tablet.

The most widely used type of dry cell is the carbon cell, or Leclanché cell, named for its inventor. Most (although not all) flashlight batteries are made up of carbon cells. Another common example is the 1 1/2-volt No. 6, the kind used to supply current to doorbells. It is one of the largest dry cells—6 inches long and

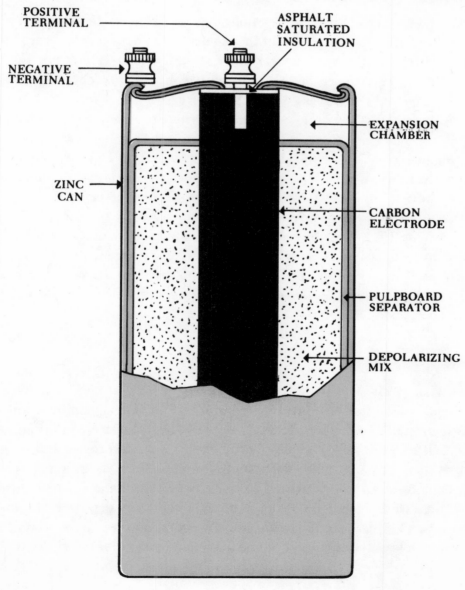

POSITIVE
TERMINAL

ASPHALT
SATURATED
INSULATION

NEGATIVE
TERMINAL

EXPANSION
CHAMBER

ZINC
CAN

CARBON
ELECTRODE

PULPBOARD
SEPARATOR

DEPOLARIZING
MIX

2 1/2 inches in diameter. An outer cardboard cylinder, closed at the bottom, holds a zinc can or cylinder that is lined with an absorbent material, much like blotting paper. Within the liner is a yellowish-white paste made up of two chemicals, ammonium chloride and zinc chloride, mixed with plaster of Paris and a small amount of water. In the center of the paste is a thick, round, black rod of carbon. Near the rod, the paste is black. This color is caused by a mixture of powdered carbon and a chemical called manganese dioxide, which is also black. The top of the zinc can is sealed by a wax or plastic disc. Between the paste and the disc is either an empty air space or a disc of spongy material that allows the paste to expand without becoming so tightly packed that the cell's chemical reactions are hampered. Protruding from the disc are two short bolts fitted with round nuts. One bolt is attached to the zinc can, the other to the carbon rod. These bolts and nuts, called *binding posts*, are convenient devices for attaching wires to the zinc and carbon.

A dry cell is not really dry. There is enough water in the paste to make it possible for chemical reactions to take place in the electrolyte. These reactions are basically the same as in a simple zinc and carbon wet cell. Negative charges (electrons) collect on the zinc can (the cathode), and positive charges collect on the carbon rod (the anode). The current leaves the cell through the binding post attached to the zinc can. Current re-enters the cell through the binding post attached to the carbon rod.

The manganese dioxide furnishes oxygen which combines with the hydrogen on the anode, forming water. Thus, the manganese dioxide is a *depolarizer*; it prevents hydrogen bubbles from forming and polarizing the cell.

As with a storage battery, a dry cell can be recharged by sending direct current into it to reverse the chemical reactions that took place when it was producing current. A dry cell can be recharged only a few times because eventually all the manganese dioxide is used up, and the cell cannot be depolarized any more. Also, the zinc can eventually is eaten away, having been used up in the electricity-producing chemical reaction.

## Fuel Cell

Modern spacecraft obtain their electric power from *fuel cells*, which are very efficient wet cells. The current is generated by chemical combination of the elements hydrogen and oxygen. The cell does not need these elements supplied in pure form, although it will work more efficiently if pure hydrogen and oxygen are supplied. A fuel cell can work with such common fuels as gasoline, kerosene, propane, or natural gas, all of which contain hydrogen. Some fuel cells use these fuels directly; others have a means of extracting the hydrogen from the fuel. The oxygen can be obtained directly from air. The combination of the hydrogen and oxygen is a chemical reaction of the kind called oxidation; the oxygen is the oxidizer.

Like other electric cells, a fuel cell contains an anode, a cathode, and an electrolyte. The electrolyte can be either an acid or a base. Fuel and oxidizer are introduced into separate compartments on opposite sides of the cell. The electrolyte surrounds the compartments. The wall of each compartment that is in contact with the electrolyte is porous. Molecules of the fuel and the oxidizer can pass through the pores in these walls. The fuel compartment is the cathode, the supplier of electrons that make up the current that leaves the cell. The oxidizer compartment is the anode, the supplier of positive charges.

A fuel cell operates continuously as long as hydrogen and oxygen are supplied. Unlike other electric cells, a fuel cell does not polarize, the electrolyte does not change, and the cell never needs charging. The products of the chemical reaction are carbon dioxide and water, which are nonpoisonous, not difficult or unpleasant to handle, and easily disposable.

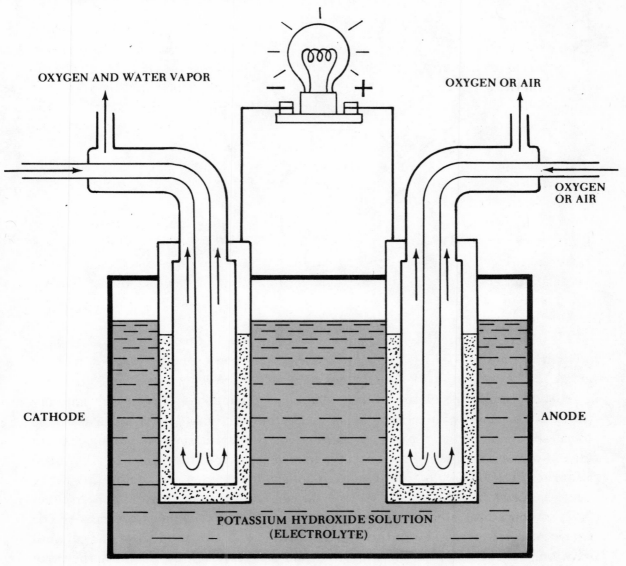

OXYGEN AND WATER VAPOR

OXYGEN OR AIR

OXYGEN OR AIR

CATHODE

ANODE

POTASSIUM HYDROXIDE SOLUTION
(ELECTROLYTE)

## Solar Cell and Battery

A solar cell changes the energy of sunlight to electrical energy. This change is based on the fact that when light strikes the atoms of certain substances, it dislodges electrons from the atoms. Actually, any light will do this, but the brighter the light, the more energy it has, and the larger the number of electrons it dislodges. Since sunlight is very bright, easily available, and free, it is used to make the light-energy-changing cell work. Since "sol" is the Latin word for sun, these cells are called *solar* cells.

To make a solar cell, a small amount of the chemical element arsenic is mixed with the element silicon. This mixture contains large numbers of free electrons. Next, a small amount of the element boron is mixed with silicon. This mixture has large numbers of empty spaces (called *holes*) where electrons are missing from their usual positions. A thin wafer of arsenic-silicon (about twenty-thousandths of an inch thick) is coated with an even thinner layer of boron-silicon.

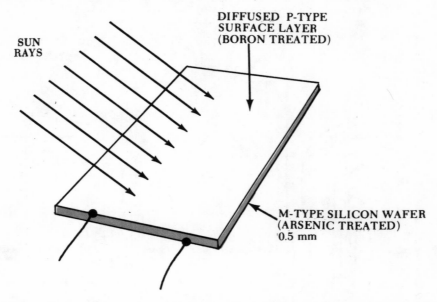

SUN RAYS

DIFFUSED P-TYPE SURFACE LAYER (BORON TREATED)

M-TYPE SILICON WAFER (ARSENIC TREATED) 0.5 mm

The surface at which the two kinds of silicon meet is called a *junction*. The junction ordinarily forms a barrier which electrons cannot cross. But when light strikes the layers of silicon, it dislodges many electrons from the atoms, creating large numbers of free electrons (negative charges) and holes (positive charges). And great numbers of electrons are driven across the junction. When wires of a circuit are connected to each of the layers, electrons flow from the arsenic-silicon side out of the cell, through the circuit, and return to the boron-silicon layer, filling the holes. The flow of electrons makes up an electric current.

A silicon cell one inch square in sunlight can generate about seven-hundredths (0.07) of a watt of electric power. Large numbers of solar cells are connected together in batteries. The output of the batteries is the total power of all the individual cells. Since solar cells need no fuel and can work indefinitely, they are especially useful on artificial satellites, where worn-out batteries cannot be charged. Certain satellites carry 3,600 solar cells, which generate more than 250 watts. When one of these satellites is passing through the earth's shadow—the night side of the earth—the satellite uses electric current from nickel-cadmium storage batteries that were charged by the solar battery when the satellite was in sunlight.

## ELECTRIC LIGHT

Electricity is used in a number of devices to produce light. The best-known and most widely used device is the electric lamp, which is used in almost every home and public building.

### Incandescent Lamp, or Electric Light Bulb

The incandescent lamp is the familiar light bulb that is used in most homes. It consists of a brass or aluminum base having a wide screw-thread with which the lamp may be secured in a socket of a lighting fixture, such as a table lamp or a chandelier. The metal base of the bulb, called a *base shell*, is a hollow cup. Rising from the base shell is a hollow glass tube called a *stem press*. Sealed into the stem press are two very thin wires that run from the base shell to the upper part of the lamp. Rising from the stem press is a thin solid glass rod, the *button rod*. The top of the rod is a flat glass "button." Sealed into this button is a very thin wire. This wire and the two that arise from the stem press support a coil of fine wire called a *filament*. The ends of the filament are connected to the ends of the two wires that arise from the base shell through the stem press. All this apparatus is contained in a glass bulb that tapers into a neck which is sealed into the base shell.

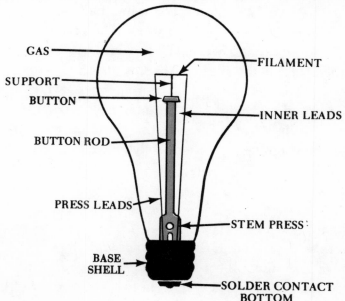

GAS — FILAMENT
SUPPORT —
BUTTON —
INNER LEADS
BUTTON ROD —
PRESS LEADS —
STEM PRESS
BASE SHELL —
SOLDER CONTACT BOTTOM

Electric current enters the bulb through a solder contact button at the bottom of the base shell. This button is separated from the base shell by a ring of insulating material that prevents the entering current from going through the metal of the base shell. The current flows up a lead-in wire, which is one of the two arising from the stem press, and then goes through the filament and down the other fine wire, which is attached to the inside of the base shell. From there, the current flows out of the lamp. The lead-in solder contact button is insulated from the rest of the base shell so that the current will flow *out* of the base.

The wire of the filament is made of the element wolfram, or tungsten, only four ten-thousandths (.0004) of an inch thick, about the size of a human hair. The wire is coiled and then the coil itself is coiled, so that the filament is actually a coiled coil. Coiling the wire makes it possible to have longer wire within that space than would be possible if the wire were straight. A filament about one inch long is made from a 30-inch length of wire. The tungsten wire has a very high melting point—about 7,000° Fahrenheit. It also has very high resistance to the flow of electric current. The current has difficulty in flowing, not only because of the wire's high resistance, but also because the wire is thin. Trying to send a large amount of current through a thin wire that has high resistance is like trying to send an immense amount of water through a thin hose with rough inside walls. Forcing the water through the hose will result in tremendous friction between the water and the hose. Forcing a stream of electrons into the filament results in a kind of electrical friction that knocks vast numbers of electrons out of the orbits of tungsten atoms. As electrons fall back into the orbits, the tungsten atoms emit (give off) heat and light. The coil of wire becomes very hot and radiates a bright white light. When a substance becomes hot enough to give off light, it is said to be *incandescent*.

Although the filament becomes quite hot, it does not burn, because burning requires the presence of oxygen. There is no oxygen in the bulb; it is filled with a mixture of gases that will not support combustion, or burning. This mixture consists of a small amount of argon in nitrogen. The presence of the argon causes the filament to glow more brightly and last longer.

The high temperature of the filament causes atoms of tungsten to boil off the wire. These collect at the top of the bulb as a dark area which you probably have seen in an old or burned-out lamp. As the filament loses atoms, the wire becomes thinner and thinner. The temperature of the thinning wire gradually increases. Eventually it becomes high enough to melt the wire, and the lamp "burns out."

## Fluorescent Lamp

A fluorescent lamp consists of a long sealed glass tube with a filament at each end. Within the tube are argon gas and a small amount of the element mercury. Baked on the inside of the tube is a coating made of a mixture of powdered fluorescent substances, called phosphors. These substances emit light when struck

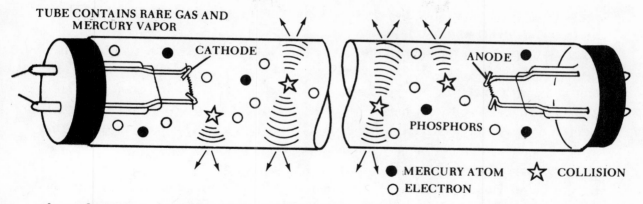

TUBE CONTAINS RARE GAS AND MERCURY VAPOR

CATHODE

ANODE

PHOSPHORS

● MERCURY ATOM ☆ COLLISION
○ ELECTRON

by radiation such as ultraviolet light—which should be called ultraviolet radiation because it is not really light; you cannot see it.

Electric current enters the tube and passes through one of the filaments, heating it to incandescence. This causes it to emit electrons at high speed. This filament is the cathode; the filament at the other end of the tube is the anode. Since the anode is charged positive, it attracts the negatively charged electrons, increasing the speed with which they fly through the tube. But since the tube uses alternating current, the cathode and anode switch roles as fast as the current changes direction, which is sixty times a second. The incandescent cathodes bombard the mercury with electrons, vaporizing it, and filling the tube with mercury atoms.

When a speeding electron collides with a mercury atom, the atom gives off radiation, which includes the ultraviolet. The phosphors absorb the ultraviolet radiation and emit their own radiation, which is light. The color of the light given off by the lamp can be varied by using different mixtures of phosphors.

Fluorescent lamps are more efficient than incandescent lamps. An incandescent lamp must generate a great deal of heat in order to cause the filament to glow. Most of the electrical energy that goes into an incandescent lamp is changed into heat energy. (This is why a light bulb becomes so hot when it is lit.) On the other hand, in a fluorescent lamp, more of the incoming energy becomes light than becomes heat.

In the United States, most public buildings, stores, and factories are lighted by fluorescent lamps. And many lighting fixtures in houses use this type of lamp. As a result, the fluorescent is the most widely used type of lamp.

## ELECTRIC APPLIANCES

### Electric Toaster

An electric toaster is based on the fact that heat is produced by an electric current flowing through metal (or any other substance having high electrical resistance). One metal that has extremely high resistance is *Nichrome,* an alloy composed of nickel and chromium.

The outer part of a toaster is a metal box. In the top of the box are openings into which you may drop two or more slices of bread *(Fig. 1).* Inside, on both sides of each slot, are panels made of asbestos, a material that is a very good insulator against heat. Passing through slits near the side of each panel, a thin flat strip of Nichrome is wound around the panel and held in place. There are about eight turns of Nichrome strip for each panel *(Fig. 2).* The strips are crimped because crimping makes it possible to fit a longer strip into a space than if the strips were straight. Some toasters use round wires instead of flat strips. In front of each panel are several vertical guide wires that keep the slices of bread from falling sideways against the Nichrome strips.

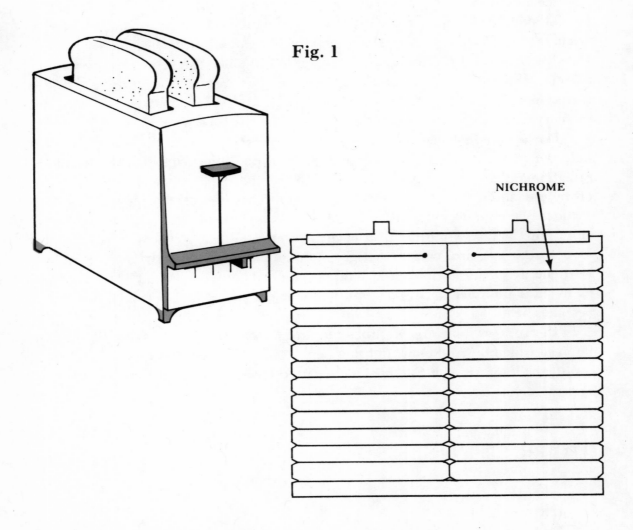

Fig. 1

NICHROME

Fig. 2

A slice of bread put into a slot rests on a support made of strips of metal. When you push down on a lever at the front of the toaster, you lower the support and the bread goes all the way down into the toaster. Depressing the lever also makes a contact that lets electric current flow into the Nichrome strips. The strips become red-hot, and the heat toasts both slices of bread on both sides.

Different makes of toasters have different arrangements for causing the finished toast to pop up halfway out of the openings at the top of the toaster. But all pop-up devices work in the same general way. When the lever is pushed down, lowering the slices of bread into the toaster, a piece of metal attached to the lever hooks beneath a catch and is held in place. The catch is attached to a bimetallic strip made of two strips of different metals fastened together along their whole lengths. As the temperature changes, the bimetallic strip bends. It bends in one direction when it is heated and in the opposite direction when it is cooled.

The longer the Nichrome strips glow red-hot, the higher the temperature rises inside the toaster. When the temperature reaches the degree of heat needed to finish toasting a slice of bread, the bimetallic strip has bent so far that it pulls the catch away from the piece of metal it has been holding. The lever is no longer hooked beneath the catch. A released spring beneath the lever pushes it, and the bread support with it, halfway up the toaster. The toast pops halfway out of the slots. The rising lever breaks the electrical contact, and the toaster is turned off.

By varying the time that the bread is in the toaster, the degree of toasting can be varied. The longer the bread is in the toaster, the darker it is toasted. To vary time, a knob, pointer, or some other kind of control is attached to the catch fastened to the bimetallic strip. By turning the knob or moving the pointer, the bimetallic strip can be bent. If the strip and its catch are bent close to the piece of metal on the lever, the bimetallic strip will have to move back farther before it unhooks the catch. Bending farther requires more heat. To reach this degree of heat takes more time. As a result, the bread is heated longer and is toasted darker.

Varying the toasting time is not the only way the degree of toasting may be varied. Some toasters have a knob or a pointer that controls the amount of electric current entering the toaster. More current results in hotter Nichrome strips or wires. And a hotter toaster means darker toast.

Many toasters have both kinds of controls. The current control sets a range of heat, and the time control makes a fine adjustment within that heat range.

## Electric Iron

The modern electric iron, used for pressing clothes, is another device that makes use of the heat produced when electric current flows through metal with high electrical resistance.

On the outside of the iron (*Fig. 1, next page*) there is a *sole plate*, which is the bottom of the iron. Resting on the sole plate and attached to it is a metal *cover*. Attached to the cover is a *handle*, usually made of a plastic that conducts heat very poorly. This keeps the ironer's hand from being burned. Attached to either cover or the handle is a *selector dial* for setting the temperature of the iron. A wire is attached to the rear of the cover. At its free end is a pronged plug for plugging the iron into an electrical outlet.

Inside the cover *(Fig. 2, next page)* is an iron plate, the *intermediate* plate, which rests on the sole plate. The intermediate plate fits into a depression molded into the sole plate, but the two plates are not fastened together, which leaves the intermediate plate free to move a little—to expand when heated and to contract when cooled. Located in a channel around the upper edge of the intermediate plate is the *heating element,* a coil of Nichrome wire.

Resting on the intermediate plate is a temperature-adjusting unit that has a metal rod with a screw thread passing upward through the cover and into the center of the temperature-selecting dial. The lower end of the rod contacts a gear—and the gear, in turn, contacts a short, toothed strip of metal. The teeth of the gear and the strip fit together. Attached to one end of the strip is a short ceramic rod.

Behind the temperature-selecting unit is an arrangement of flat metal springs. One spring is made of a strip of Invar, a metal that expands and contracts very little as its temperature changes. The Invar strip is bent in the middle, and a metallic connecting rod passes through a hole in the bend. The ends of the strip are

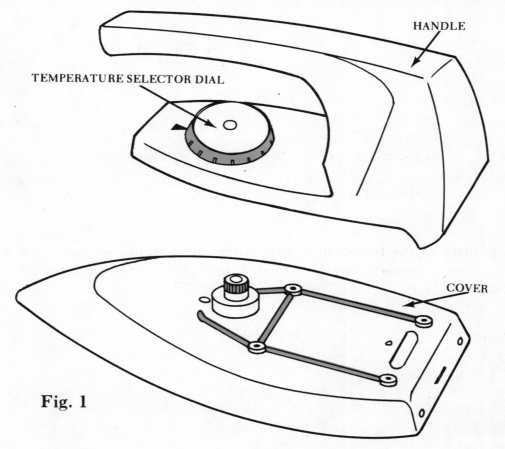

HANDLE

TEMPERATURE SELECTOR DIAL

COVER

Fig. 1

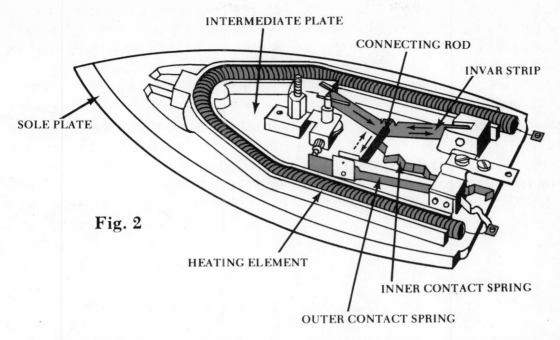

INTERMEDIATE PLATE

CONNECTING ROD

INVAR STRIP

SOLE PLATE

**Fig. 2**

HEATING ELEMENT

INNER CONTACT SPRING

OUTER CONTACT SPRING

held in slots in molded raised parts of the intermediate plate. The strip can buckle forward or backward (*note arrows in Fig. 2*) as the intermediate plate expands or contracts. Buckling moves the connecting rod forward or backward. The rod is attached to a zigzag strip of metal, the *inner contact spring*. One end of this spring is attached to the connecting rod at the middle of its length, and the other end pushes against a straight strip of metal, the *outer contact spring*. This spring can move so as to push against the ceramic rod. The inner and outer contact springs act as a switch that either lets electric current into the heating element or turns the current off.

On the temperature-selector dial are markings variously labeled WOOL, COTTON, NYLON, SILK, etc., that indicate ironing temperatures. Each one indicates that if the dial is set at a designated mark, the iron will heat to a temperature high enough for ironing that particular fabric, but not so hot as to scorch or burn it.

Suppose you have chosen a setting on the dial. The heating element will heat the sole plate to the temperature that is best for ironing the fabric you have chosen. At this temperature the expanding intermediate plate will have moved enough to bend the Invar strip in the direction that will lengthen it. The strip will buckle outward, pulling on the connecting rod. The rod will pull on the inner contact spring. The outer contact spring will follow the inner contact spring until the outer spring strikes the end of the ceramic rod. This rod will prevent the outer contact spring from following the inner spring any farther. The inner spring will then move away from the outer spring, breaking the circuit, and cutting off electric current from the heating element. The distance the outer contact spring can move depends on how far the ceramic rod has been moved by your adjustment of the temperature-selector dial.

When the current is cut off, the iron begins to cool. The Invar strip now buckles inward. The movements of the inner and outer contact springs are now the reverse of what they were when the iron was heating. As a result, electrical contact is remade, and electric current again flows into the heating element.

Some electric irons are called steam irons, which emit steam through holes in the sole plate. Some fabrics are best ironed when they are damp. Steam enables the ironer to dampen fabrics without having to sprinkle them with water by hand, before ironing begins.

Steam irons have a reservoir of water inside the cover. When the dial is set at STEAM, water flows out of an outlet in the reservoir and into channels in the sole plate. The hot sole plate turns the water to steam, which escapes from the holes in the sole plate.

## Electric Fan

An electric fan consists of angled blades fastened to the shaft of an electric motor. As the armature of the motor turns the shaft, the revolving blades push air outward from the front of the fan, creating a breeze. The motor itself is enclosed in a metallic housing and mounted on a stand.

As the blades turn, each one strikes and pushes on the air in its path. Since the blades are mounted at an angle, the air slides off a blade at the same angle that the blade is set in the shaft. As a result, the air moves in a direction parallel to the shaft.

The fan's blades are usually made of metal and are surrounded by a cage of heavy wire, designed to prevent anyone from accidentally touching the whirling blades and being badly cut. Some electric fans have soft-rubber blades that will not hurt a person who touches them when they are spinning.

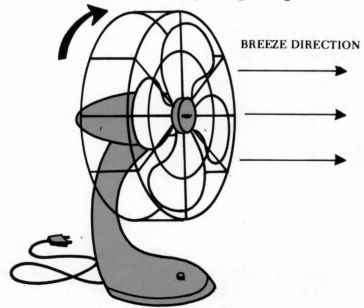

BREEZE DIRECTION

Many kinds of fans turn slowly back and forth, spreading the breeze to an area of 180 degrees (half a circle) or more. There is more than one way to create this slow back-and-forth motion. The fan is mounted so that it can turn, while the stand remains stationary. Power for the back-and-forth motion is provided by the same motor that turns the fan. An arrangement of gears slows down the turning speed of the shaft of the motor. The gears also transform the turning motion of the shaft to a circular back-and-forth motion that moves the whole fan.

## Vacuum Cleaner

A vacuum cleaner is a machine that employs a high-speed electric fan to remove dirt, grit, small pieces of thread, paper, wood, and other materials by carrying them in a stream of air through a nozzle and into a bag.

There are two types of vacuum cleaners, the *upright*, and the *canister*. The upright type *(see illustration below)* is a long-handled metal or plastic airtight container which holds a bag for catching dirt, a dust filter, a fan and an electric motor. At the floor level, the handle is attached to a wide metal or plastic housing, or cover, inside of which a rotating brush is driven by a belt from the motor. The brush, striking against the pile fibers of rugs, dislodges dirt that is then carried up into the bag. The entire upright vacuum cleaner rests on wheels and is pushed and pulled over the area to be cleaned.

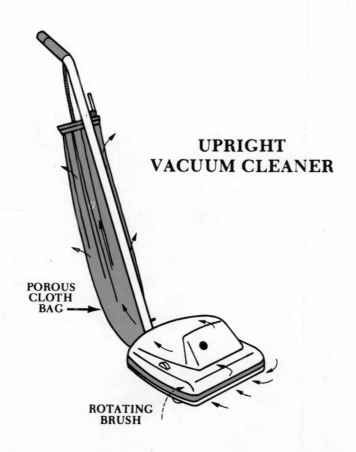

**UPRIGHT VACUUM CLEANER**

POROUS CLOTH BAG

ROTATING BRUSH

There is a small type of upright vacuum cleaner called an electric broom. The long-handled container and all the parts it houses are smaller than those of the standard upright. Instead of a rotating brush, the electric broom has simply a single nozzle under its cover that is slid back and forth over the area to be cleaned.

In a canister-type of vacuum cleaner, the dust bag, filter, fan, and motor are within an airtight, wheeled container, the canister. Attached to the canister is a long plastic hose, often covered with fabric. At the free end of the hose is a nozzle. Several different kinds of nozzles may be attached to the hose, each one being best for a particular kind of cleaning. There are nozzles for cleaning rugs, floors, fabric, and also for dusting and for cleaning narrow crevices. The nozzle for cleaning rugs may have its own rotating brush for dislodging dirt from pile fibers. This brush is rotated by a separate small motor that is in the nozzle. The canister can be wheeled about as the nozzle is moved over the area to be cleaned.

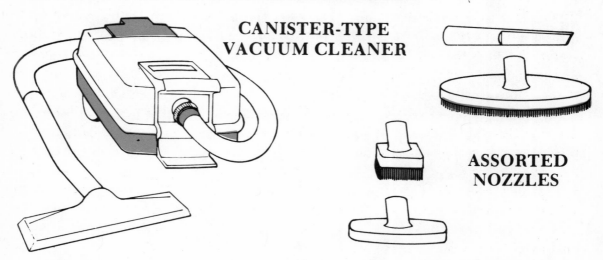

**CANISTER-TYPE VACUUM CLEANER**

**ASSORTED NOZZLES**

All types of vacuum cleaners work the same way. An electric motor inside an airtight container drives a fan with a large number of blades. The fan propels air out of a hole in the container. The pressure of the atmosphere pushes air into the container to replace the air expelled by the fan. Since the container is airtight and the only openings (except for the one out of which the air is propelled) are either at the floor-level covering or at the nozzle, the incoming air must pass through one of these two inlets. The incoming stream of air carries dust and small objects, directly or through a hose, into a paper bag fitted into the container. The fibers of the paper bag have many small spaces between them. Air escapes from the bag through these spaces, leaving behind the dust particles and other dirt that is too large to pass through these spaces. When the bag becomes filled with dust and other dirt, it is removed from the cleaner, thrown away, and replaced by a new empty bag. Some older models of vacuum cleaners use fabric bags instead of paper ones. When a fabric bag becomes full, the dust is dumped out, and the same bag is reused.

Having passed through the bag, the air is still inside the container. It passes through a filter that removes dust and grit fine enough to have passed through the bag. From the filter, the air goes through the blades of the fan, then past the motor (which usually is sealed off from the stream of air), and finally out of the container.

You can remove the hose from most models of canister vacuum cleaners and then attach it to the air outlet. Now, when the motor is turned on, air is blown out through the hose. Blowing air into narrow places will sometimes dislodge dust that cannot be pulled into the vacuum cleaner by inrushing air.

It is important to understand that a vacuum cleaner does not suck or draw air into the dust-collecting bag. The air is *pushed* into the cleaner by atmospheric pressure.

## Flashlight

A flashlight has a plastic or metal case that holds a battery of one to five dry cells. The battery provides current for an incandescent lamp, the flashlight bulb. This bulb is usually screwed into a socket in the center of a reflector. At the front of the reflector is a flat piece of glass to protect the bulb, or a glass lens for either spreading or concentrating the light of the bulb. A switch turns the current from the battery on and off, and strips of metal act as part of an electric circuit.

In a flashlight's dry cell, the anode (the positive electrode into which electric current flows) is a carbon rod tipped with a brass cap, which is at the center of the cell. The cathode (the negative electrode out of which current flows) is the bottom of the cell where the zinc container is uncovered.

Let us see how a flashlight using two dry cells works. At the rear of the case is either a coiled spring or a spring made of a flat piece of metal. The spring pushes the rear cell against the front one. The brass cap on the anode of the rear cell is held tightly in contact with the cathode, the bottom, of the front cell. And the brass cap on the front cell is held tightly against the contact button on the bottom of the flashlight bulb. Attached to the inside of the case, and running along its whole length, is a strip of metal that makes contact with the spring at the rear. In the middle of the length of the case, the metal strip is interrupted by a gap that is part of a switch. The switch may have a slider you push forward and back, or it may

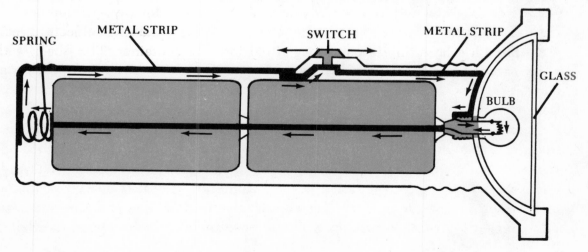

have two push-buttons, one for switching the flashlight on and one for switching it off. Whichever type of switch is used, once the flashlight is switched on, it remains lit until it is switched off.

When the flashlight is off, the switch is open. When you close the switch by moving the slider or pushing a button, you close the gap in the metal strip inside the case. Current flows from the cathode of the rear cell to the spring at the rear of the flashlight. From the spring, current flows forward through the metal strip, through the switch, and continues along the strip to the bottom of the reflector. The reflector is usually made of metal, providing a path for the current to follow to the screw socket in the reflector. Current which enters the brass base of the bulb flows up a thin wire inside the bulb to one end of the filament. Current flowing through the coiled filament causes it to glow brightly, and the bulb is lit. Current leaving the filament travels down a wire to the contact button at the bottom of the bulb, and from there to the brass cap on the anode of the front dry cell. Then it moves through the chemicals in the cell to the container, which is the cathode. The current continues out the bottom of the cell and into the brass cap (anode) of the rear cell, flowing through the chemicals to the cathode, where the current began its round trip. The circuit is complete.

There are many different arrangements of cells and bulb in various types of flashlights. The cells of the battery may be side by side. The reflector may be made of plastic which does not conduct electric current, so a strip of metal along the bottom of the reflector touches the contact button of the bulb. Wires inside the case may be used as part of the circuit. Regardless of the arrangement, the path of the current—the circuit—is the same.

## Fuses and Circuit Breakers

A *fuse* is a device that prevents too much current from flowing through an electrical circuit. An amount of current that is too great for a circuit is called an *overload*.

Suppose you connect a toaster, a refrigerator, a lamp and a television set to a single electrical wall outlet. If you turn them all on at the same time, the amount of current needed is equal to the sum of the amount of current required by each appliance. This probably will be more current than can be carried safely by the wires running through the walls to the outlet. In other words, there will be a current overload. Think of the wire as a garden hose and the current as water flowing through it. If you try to force into a garden hose as much water as flows through a fire hose in the same amount of time, the pressure will increase so much that the garden hose will burst. If you force an overload of current through a wire, the wire will not burst, but it will become hot. When too many electrical appliances all demand current at the same time, the wire carrying the incoming current may become so hot that it could melt the insulation around the wire. The hot wires without insulation could set fire to the wall. This is why a fuse is needed.

A fuse has in it a piece of metal that melts at a temperature far below the amount of heat needed to melt the insulation on a wire or to set woodwork afire. If an overload of current begins to heat the wires of a circuit in which there is a fuse, the piece of metal in the fuse melts before the wires become very hot. The melted metal drips to the bottom of the fuse, opening a gap in the circuit. Therefore, no more current can flow through the wires, and so they do not become hot enough to cause a fire. When a fuse melts, we say it "blows" or "blows out."

### CARTRIDGE FUSE

There are two main kinds of fuses: the *cartridge* and the *screw-plug*. The cartridge fuse *(above)* has a hollow cylinder made of a material that does not burn and does not conduct electricity. The ends of the cylinder are closed by metal caps. Inside the cylinder, reaching from cap to cap, is a strip of metal that does not have a very high melting point. The cartridge is held in place by two clamps of springy metal that fit around the caps. The clamps are part of the electric circuit; electric current enters the fuse through one clamp and leaves through the other. Cartridge fuses are old-fashioned, but many are still being used.

The screw-plug fuse *(below)* looks somewhat like the lower part of an electric light bulb; in fact, one common type of screw-plug fuse has exactly the same type of metal base shell. Set into the base shell is a cup-like container made of a ceramic material such as porcelain. This container sticks out about half an inch from the base, and widens near the end. Another type of screw-plug fuse has its base and protruding part both molded in one piece from a ceramic material. Both types are capped by a metal ring that has a circular window. The window is made of mica, a transparent mineral, or of plastic that does not burn easily. At the bottom of the fuse is a metal contact button. Screw-plug fuses screw into sockets like those into which electric light bulbs fit.

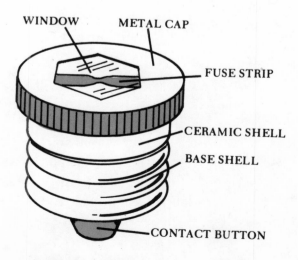

WINDOW    METAL CAP

FUSE STRIP

CERAMIC SHELL

BASE SHELL

CONTACT BUTTON

### PLUG FUSE

Inside the ceramic container is the fuse strip. The middle of this strip is much narrower than the rest. This thin and narrow bit of metal is the section that melts when an overload occurs in the circuit the fuse is protecting. One end of the fuse strip is fastened inside the fuse to the contact button. The other end of the strip passes through the wall of the ceramic container and is fastened either to the metal base shell or to a band of metal wrapped around the fuse. Either of these makes contact with the side of the socket, and the contact button makes contact with the bottom of the socket.

Looking into the window at the front of the fuse, you can see whether it has blown. If the metal strip has melted and parted, or if the window is blackened as if scorched, the fuse has blown out.

When a refrigerator is plugged in and an air-conditioner, washing machine or some other electrical appliance with a motor is turned on, an extra amount of current is needed for a moment to get the motor started. (The motor may need five times as much current to start it as when it is running.) The extra current may temporarily overload the circuit, and this temporary overload may blow a fuse. Since the overload lasts only a second or two, it is harmless; it will not heat the circuit dangerously hot. So the blowing of the fuse does not really protect the circuit from fire. Instead, the blown fuse is simply an annoyance. To get around this annoyance, a *time-delay*, or *slow-blow*, fuse (*below*) may be used.

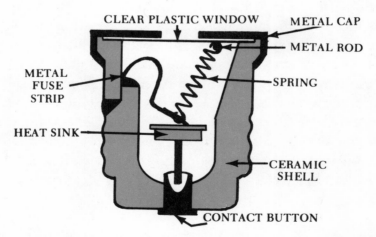

Inside the ceramic shell of a time-delay fuse, a metal rod projects upward from the contact button, rising about one-fourth of the distance to the window. Supported on top of the rod is a small brass or aluminum cup filled with a solder-like metal that can absorb heat very well. When this metal has absorbed a certain amount of heat, it melts. The metal-filled cup is called a *heat sink*. One end of a fuse strip is embedded in the heat sink. The strip may be bent so that it is springy. The other end of the fuse strip fits into a slot in the wall of the ceramic shell, and runs through to the outside. As in the regular type of screw-plug fuse, the metallic strip has a narrow part. A thin metal rod extends across the top of the inside of the fuse. One end of a spring is looped around the rod; the other end is looped around the bottom of the fuse strip. The spring is stretched, so that it is under tension.

If a heavy overload of current occurs for only a few seconds, the heat sink absorbs the heat produced by the overload. This prevents the increased heat from melting the fuse strip. The fuse, of course, does not blow, and when the overload is past, the heat sink cools and is ready for another overload. It is because the fuse can absorb the heat of an overload for several seconds that it is called a time-delay, or slow-blow, fuse. If the heavy overload occurs for more than a few seconds, or if a moderate overload occurs for several minutes, the metal in the heat sink melts. The spring then pulls the end of the fuse strip out of the molten metal. This opens a gap in the circuit, and the fuse has blown.

If a very heavy and sudden overload of current occurs, the metal in the heat sink might not melt quickly enough to prevent a large amount of current from passing through the fuse and damaging appliances connected in the circuit. If this should happen, the narrow part of the fuse strip melts, and the fuse blows with practically no delay.

Each room in a house or apartment may have its own fuse, and also each large appliance, such as a refrigerator, washer, dryer, and air conditioner. Thus, when one fuse blows out, electric current is not necessarily cut off from other rooms and appliances.

Replacing a blown fuse can be dangerous. This task should be left to adults who know how to do it. And since replacing any kind of blown fuse is a nuisance, modern buildings use *circuit breakers* instead of fuses.

There are two types of circuit breakers, *electromagnetic* and *thermal*. The first type *(below)* uses an electromagnet, a kind of magnet that works only when electric current flows through it. Like all other magnets, an electromagnet pulls toward itself objects made of iron and certain alloys. One of the things upon which the strength of an electromagnet depends is the amount of current flowing through a coil of wire that is part of the magnet. The stronger the current, the stronger the pull of the electromagnet.

An iron plunger is held in place partway within the hole in the center of the coil. A series of levers connects the electromagnet with a catch. A spring is attached to each arm of the catch. The springs hold the hooked ends of the two arms tightly together, forming the catch.

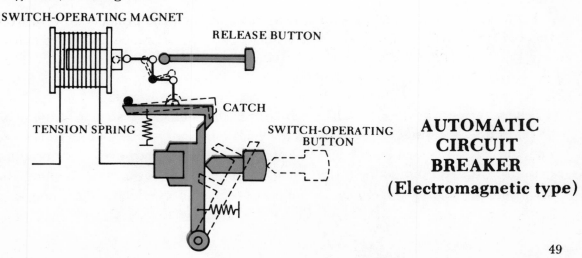

SWITCH-OPERATING MAGNET

RELEASE BUTTON

CATCH

TENSION SPRING

SWITCH-OPERATING
BUTTON

**AUTOMATIC
CIRCUIT
BREAKER
(Electromagnetic type)**

A circuit breaker is connected directly into a circuit, so that current flows through it before going to a refrigerator, a lamp, a television set, or any other electrical appliances. When the normal load of current is flowing, the pull of the electromagnet is not strong enough to open the catch. When an overload occurs, the strength of the electromagnet increases greatly, pulling the plunger all the way into the hole in the coil. The movement of the electromagnet causes the levers to push open the catch. The two springs now act to pull the two arms far apart and hold the catch wide open. (The dotted figure shows the positions of the parts of the circuit breaker after the catch has opened.) The open catch is a break in the circuit which stops the flow of current, preventing the overload from doing any harm.

The thermal circuit breaker (below) uses the heat produced by the current overload. *Thermal* means "having to do with heat." The thermal circuit breaker has the same parts as the electromagnetic type, except for two things. One of them is a coil of wire with high electrical resistance, located where the current enters the circuit breaker. The other part is a bimetallic strip, made by fastening strips of two different kinds of metal together lengthwise. When the temperature of a bimetallic strip is changed, the strip bends. The bimetallic strip is located in the center of the coil. An arrangement of levers is attached to the bimetallic strip.

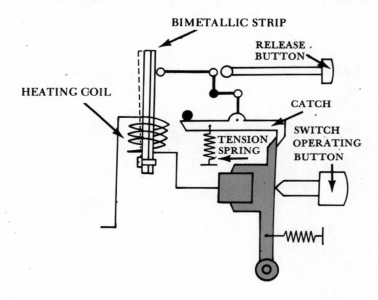

## AUTOMATIC CIRCUIT BREAKER
### (Thermal type)

When current flows through wire with high electrical resistance, the wire becomes hot. A normal load of current does not produce enough heat in the coil of a circuit breaker to bend the bimetallic strip. An overload, however, does produce enough heat. The bimetallic strip bends, pulling on the levers and pushing the catch open. This breaks the circuit and prevents the overload from doing any harm.

Up to this point, the circuit breakers have accomplished the same safety function as fuses. The difference is that, with a circuit breaker, once you have corrected the cause of the overload, all you need do is push a reset button and the circuit will be completed again. Pushing the reset button moves the hooked ends of the two arms into position so that they link up the way they were before.

Suppose an electrician wants to fix an electrical wall outlet. It would be dangerous to do any work on the outlet if current could flow through it. One way to cut off the current would be to remove from the fuse box the fuse that protects the wires running to the wall outlet. But if there is a circuit breaker instead of a fuse, the electrician need only push a release button to break the circuit. A push on the button moves the levers in the same way as when the electromagnet pulls on them.

# ELECTRONICS

Radio and television sets are two electronic machines you probably know best. You have turned them on and tuned them in. In plugging them into an electrical outlet or putting batteries of electric dry cells into them, you must have realized that there is a connection between electronics and electricity. Let us see what this connection is and how electronic machines work.

In electricity, great numbers of electrons move through wires and other devices made of metal, a material which conducts electricity very well—that is to say, the electrons pass through metal very easily. In electronics, electrons move through empty space, which does not conduct electricity at all; in other words, the electrons move through materials that ordinarily are not conductors of electricity. This type of movement is called *electron emission*. It is mainly used to control the flow of electric current. Electronics makes possible very delicate and precise control of electric current.

## ELECTRON TUBES AND RADIOS

The first electronic device was the *electron tube*. For more than fifty years it was practically the only electronic device that was widely used. Electron tubes made possible radio and television communication, radar, sonar, radiophoto transmission, and many other machines and processes that are a part of modern living. The history of the electron tube and radio broadcasting gives us a good explanation of how both work.

## Edison's Bulb

The first electron tube was made accidentally by the American inventor, Thomas A. Edison, in 1883. Edison, who invented the electric incandescent lamp, was searching for a way to keep the carbon filament of his lamp from blackening the glass bulb. The heat of the glowing filament was vaporizing the carbon; it boiled carbon atoms off the filament and they collected on the glass, darkening it. Edison hoped that by putting a metal plate inside the bulb the carbon atoms would collect on the plate instead of the glass. He placed the plate a little above and to the side of the filament *(see illustration)*. He attached to the plate a wire than ran through the wall of the bulb and was connected to an *ammeter*, an instrument for measuring electric current. The ammeter was connected to the circuit that sent current to the filament of the lamp. The wire was sealed into the glass and as much air as possible was withdrawn from the bulb.

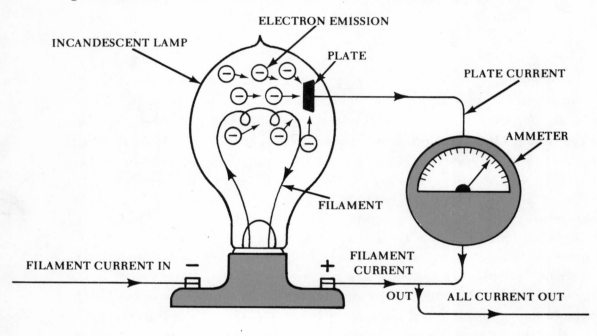

When current was sent through the filament, Edison found that the ammeter registered a small amount of current. This surprised him because the ammeter, wire, and plate did not form a circuit—a round-trip path—for electric current. Edison also found that current flowed only when the ammeter and plate were connected to the positive terminal of the electric battery that was supplying current to the filament. When he reversed the current so that the ammeter and plate were connected to the negative terminal of the battery, no current flowed through the ammeter.

Edison did not understand what was happening. He thought his electric-light bulb with a plate inside might be used to measure voltage. He patented his device, showed a few models to scientists, and abandoned it.

Today we can explain the strange behavior of Edison's lamp. The heat of the filament not only boiled off some atoms of carbon, but also vast numbers of electrons from carbon atoms that remained as parts of the filament. These electrons, which were negative electric charges, left behind on the filament carbon atoms that had more protons than electrons. Since the protons were positive charges, the atoms were positively charged. Also, since positive and negative charges attract, the electrons were pulled back to the filament before they had moved very far. This was the situation before the metal plate was put into the bulb.

When the plate was placed in the bulb near the filament, and was connected to the positive terminal of the battery, the plate was charged positive. When the positive charge on the plate became stronger than the positive charge on the filament, the plate attracted the electrons that would have been pulled back to the filament. Once on the plate, the electrons moved through the wire as an electric current, which registered on the ammeter. When Edison charged the plate negative, it had the same kind of charge as the electrons—and repelled, rather than attracted, any that came near. No current, then, flowed through the wire and none registered on the ammeter.

When electric current is sent into any thin wire, especially one made from metal that has high resistance to the passage of electric current, the wire glows red-hot or white-hot; it becomes incandescent. The incoming electrons crowding past the atoms of which the wire is made give up a large amount of energy. Some is in the form of heat or light, and some causes electrons to fly out of the orbits of the atoms. The atoms are said to *emit* the electrons, in a process called *electron emission*. The object—usually the filament—emitting the electrons is called an *emitter*.

Edison's invention might have remained as just one more unsuccessful experiment, if scientists had not been trying to find a way to broadcast the human voice and other sounds. The efforts of these scientists eventually resulted in radio broadcasting. As their experiments progressed, scientists realized that Edison's bulb-and-plate device could be a big step toward their goal. To understand what these experimenters were doing, you must understand two terms used by radio engineers: *wavelength* and *frequency*.

## Wavelength and Frequency

If you have ever thrown a stone into water, you have seen the rings that move outward from the spot where the stone struck the water *(Fig. 1)*. The rings are waves of water—up-and-down *movements* of water spreading outward from a center. The waves are not made up of water traveling outward; it is only the up-and-down movement that travels outward. You can prove this by throwing a small stick into water and then tossing a stone near the stick. As each water wave passes, the stick will move up and down; then the wave will pass it by. If the wave were made up of water moving outward, it would carry the stick along with it.

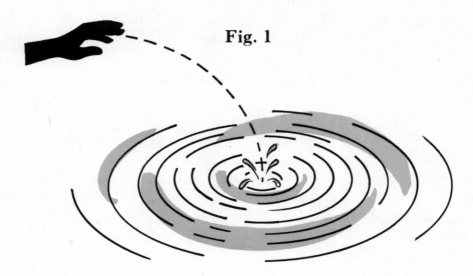

**Fig. 1**

To get a better idea of what waves are like, tie a length of clothesline to a doorknob. Hold the free end of the clothesline in one hand and step back from the door just far enough so that the lowest part of the clothesline is about an inch off the floor. Now, move your hand rapidly up and down *(Fig. 2)*. The rope will form itself into a series of hills and valleys. It will look as if the rope is moving into the doorknob, but of course you know that it is not, since you are holding the other end of it. The hills and valleys look much the way the waves on the surface of water would look if you could slice straight down through the water and look at the slice from the side.

Now, imagine a line drawn from your hand to the doorknob, halfway between the tops of the hills and the bottoms of the valleys. This line will be a guide for measuring the waves of rope. The distance measured along the line between the beginning of one hill and the beginning of the next hill is one *wavelength.* The

**Fig. 2**

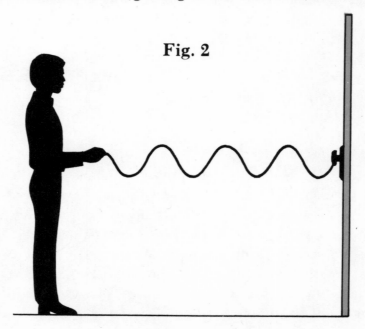

wavelength also could have been measured between the tops of two consecutive hills, the bottoms of two consecutive valleys, or any similar points of two consecutive rope waves.

Choose a point between your hand and the doorknob. Then measure the number of wavelengths that pass that point in a period of time, such as one second. This number will be the *frequency* of the waves *(Fig. 3)*. Suppose that exactly one wavelength passes in one second; then the frequency of the rope waves is one wave per second. If you will now move your hand up and down twice as fast, you will find that two waves pass our chosen point each second. The frequency of the waves has increased to two per second. Scientists call one complete wave a *cycle*. A cycle is an event that takes place over and over again, always returning to its beginning. This is what a wave does; it goes from, let us say, the bottom of a valley to a peak and then back to the bottom of a valley. One wavelength per second is one cycle per second; ten wavelengths per second are ten cycles per second.

## Fig. 3

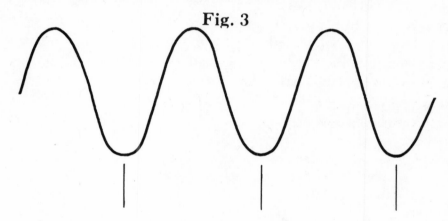

We need learn just one more term before going on with the story of electron tubes and radio. Think of the line we drew halfway between the tops and bottoms of the rope waves. The distance from this line to the top of any wave (or the bottom of any wave) is the *amplitude* of the wave.

## Radio Waves

You no doubt have heard of radio waves. A more scientific name for them is *electromagnetic waves*. Whenever an electric charge moves suddenly, it broadcasts electromagnetic waves. These waves have frequencies that vary from thousands of cycles per second to hundreds of billions of billions of cycles per second. Radio waves vary from thousands per second to tens of billions per second. All electromagnetic waves travel at a speed of 186,000 miles per second.

It was in 1856 that the idea of electromagnetic waves was first conceived. James Clerk Maxwell, a young English physicist, worked out a set of mathematical equations in which he predicted that whenever there is movement of the electric charges that cause an electromagnetic field, electromagnetic waves are produced.

Thirty-two years later, a young German physicist, Heinrich R. Hertz, proved by experiment that Maxwell's electromagnetic waves actually existed. He reasoned that if a moving electric charge could produce electromagnetic waves, then a device similar to the one that produced the charges should be able to change the waves back to electric charges.

Using step-up transformers, Hertz generated a strong electric current that was able to jump the gap between two knobs on the ends of metal rods. The spark was made up of moving electric charges. Hertz also made a metal ring with a gap and knobs *(see illustration)*. Holding the ring several feet from the spark generator, Hertz found that when sparks jumped the gap at the generator, sparks immediately jumped the gap in the ring. No wires or anything else connected the spark generator and the ring. (In terms used in modern radio engineering, the spark generator was the *transmitter*, and the ring was the *receiver*.) Hertz concluded that the electromagnetic waves theorized by Maxwell were carrying electrical energy from the generator to the ring. One of the honors bestowed upon Hertz for his discovery was to name after him the radio-engineering unit of one cycle per second—the *hertz*, abbreviated *hz*. If a radio station is broadcasting waves at a frequency of one million cycles per second, we say they are broadcasting at one million hertz, or 1,000,000 hz.

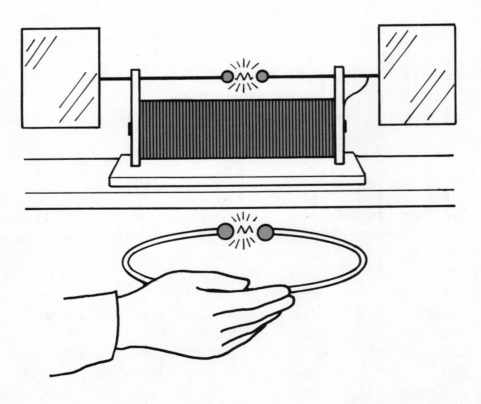

## Wireless

After Hertz's discovery, many scientists tried to find ways to broadcast electromagnetic waves over long distances. The first to succeed was a young Italian-Irish electrical engineer, Guglielmo Marconi, who connected one side of a spark gap to a wire that led to tall poles with wires strung between them. These were the first antennae. He connected the other side of the spark gap to a wire in the ground. This means that the free end of the wire was attached to a conductor of electricity, such as a flat metal plate, and the plate was buried in the ground.

In 1901, using this apparatus, Marconi was able to broadcast from England electromagnetic waves that caused sparks to jump a gap in Newfoundland, on the other side of the Atlantic Ocean. Marconi named his apparatus the "wireless," to distinguish it from the telephone and the telegraph, both of which sent electric energy over wires. Soon Marconi had wireless apparatus that could broadcast electromagnetic waves and produce a thousand sparks per second in a spark gap any distance away on earth. This great number of sparks made a high-pitched whine. By interrupting the whine—making it last for shorter or longer periods—wireless operators produced a series of short "beeps" (dots) and long "beeps" (dashes) which were combined in different ways to form a code. This came to be known as the International Morse Code. Messages could be broadcast by using code letters to spell out the words.

Marconi contributed to radio broadcasting by showing how to broadcast electromagnetic waves over long distances. But his wireless was electric, not electronic.

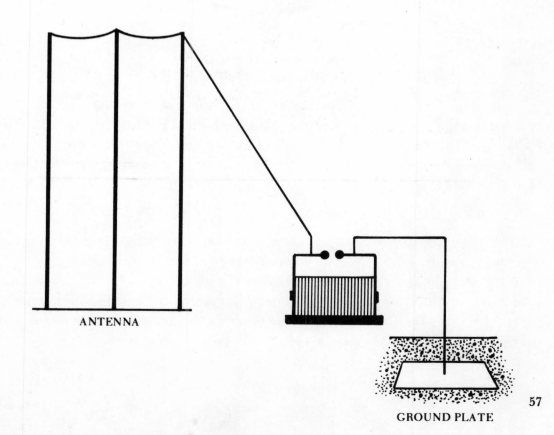

ANTENNA

GROUND PLATE

57

## Electron Tube

An English electrical engineer, John Ambrose Fleming, who was chief technical advisor for Marconi's wireless company, happened to acquire one of Edison's plate-in-a-bulb devices. Fleming thought Edison's device might be used to receive broadcast electromagnetic waves. After years of working on this idea (though abandoning it several times), Fleming, in 1904, got the device to work quite well. Instead of using a flat plate, he surrounded the filament with a cylindrical plate.

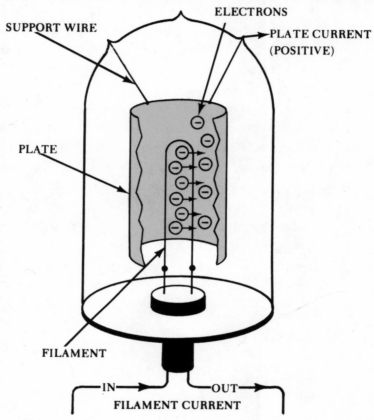

By this arrangement, electrons would be attracted to the plate as they were emitted from all sides of the filament. This device was the first true electron tube. Fleming called it a "valve," and in Britain, ever since, electron tubes have been called valves. When we learn how a radio works, we shall understand why Fleming chose this name.

## Alternating Current Waves

Attempts to broadcast voices, music and other sounds by means of a Marconi wireless transmitter failed. A thousand sparks per second in the spark gap did not produce electromagnetic waves of frequency high enough to carry sound. In the year 1900, an American electrical engineer, Reginald Aubrey Fessenden, managed to broadcast his voice for a distance of one mile by using a spark generator that produced 20,000 sparks per second. Then he decided to eliminate the spark generator. He reasoned that alternating electric current should produce electromagnetic waves, and that each time the current changed direction and returned to its original direction, one complete wave should be broadcast.

After much technical trouble, an alternating-current generator that could produce a current that changed direction 200,000 times per second was built. It produced electromagnetic waves with a frequency of 100,000 cycles per second, or hertzes. With this generator, Fessenden broadcast music and a reading from the Bible on Christmas Eve, 1906. His broadcast, from Brant Rock on the Massachusetts coast near Boston, was heard by ships at sea as far south as the Virginia coast. A year later, Fessenden was broadcasting all the way across the Atlantic Ocean.

Besides overcoming the problem of distance, Fessenden had shown that simple alternating current can produce electromagnetic waves for use in radio broadcasting.

## Triode

Following close on Fleming's heels, Lee De Forest, an electrical engineer in the United States, felt that Fleming's valve could be improved. De Forest thought there should be a way to control the electron emission—to make it as strong or weak as needed. To the U. S. Patent Office he submitted a number of designs for the kind of electron tube he wanted. One hit the mark. In it he placed, between the filament and the plate, a zigzag of thin wire, called a *grid. (See illustration below.)* This produced the results De Forest was seeking. He had invented the electron tube, which not only made modern radio communication possible, but also marked the beginning of the Electronic Age.

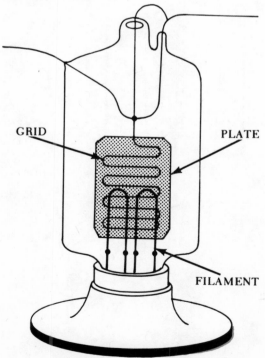

GRID      PLATE

FILAMENT

Engineers call De Forest's electron tube a *triode*. *Tri* means "three," and refers to the tube's three main working parts, the emitter, the plate, and the grid. *Ode* comes from a Greek word meaning "path" or "way." So a triode is a three-way device.

In a modern triode *(see illustration below)*, the filament is not used directly as the emitter of electrons. Instead, the filament is surrounded by a narrow sleeve made of a metal that gives off large numbers of electrons when heated. This metal sleeve is heated by the incandescent filament and emits the electrons that travel to the plate. The sleeve and the filament together make up the emitter. The grid is not a simple zigzag of wire, but a spiral of wire that surrounds the emitter. The plate surrounds the grid. As much air as possible is removed from the glass bulb, and a small amount of argon gas is put into it. The base of the tube is made of a tough plastic. The working parts of the tube are connected to the circuits of the radio set, television set, or other device in which the tube is being used, by pins—short metal rods projecting downward from the bottom of the base. Most modern electron tubes have more parts than a triode, but the added parts are there to make the three basic parts—emitter, grid, and plate—work better.

Since the emitter is the source of electrons, it is the cathode, or negative electrode. The electrons move to the plate, which then is the anode, or positive electrode.

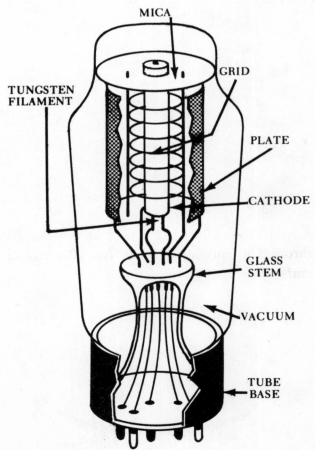

## Triode as Amplifier

In the triode, electric current sent through the filament heats it, and the metal sleeve emits electrons. As in the case of Edison's invention, if the plate is charged negative, it will repel the emitted electrons, and no current will flow out of the wire connected to the plate. If, on the other hand, the plate is charged positive, it will attract the emitted electrons and a current will flow from the plate. The more current we put into the filament, the hotter it will become, and the more electrons will fly off the emitter. This will increase the current flowing from the plate—up to a certain point. This point, the saturation point, occurs when a cloud of electrons forms on the plate and repels arriving electrons. This is where the grid does its work. Suppose the grid is charged negative. It will repel the emitted electrons. And now suppose that we send current into the grid so that it is charged positive. It will attract electrons, and most of them will pass through the grid like a swarm of flies through a wire fence. Once through the grid, the electrons will continue traveling to the plate.

Knowing what the grid will do, scientists construct the following circuit: they keep the plate charged positive; they make sure that the filament is not so hot that it will cause the plate current to reach the point of saturation; and finally, they charge the grid positive. The result is that increased current flows out of the plate without increasing the current flowing into the filament. In other words, the grid increases, or *amplifies*, the current sent into the filament. This is how an electron tube can act as an *amplifier*.

## Triode as Current Controller

Since the grid can be charged either negative or positive, we can connect it into a circuit that makes it possible to vary the grid current from very negative to less negative, then to positive and very positive. As a result, the amount of electrons that travel from the emitter to the plate range from none at all to great numbers. This means that the plate current can be varied from none at all to a great amount.

We can better understand the working of a grid by comparing it to a Venetian blind. When its slats are wide open, practically no light is stopped by the blind; almost all passes through it. Similarly, when the grid has its strongest positive charge, almost all emitted electrons pass through it.

As the slats of the Venetian blind are gradually closed, less light passes through; more of the light is blocked by the slats. Similarly, as the charge on the grid gradually changes from positive to negative, fewer and fewer electrons pass through; more and more are repelled by an increasingly negative charge.

When the Venetian blind is completely closed, no light passes through; and when the grid is charged most strongly negative, no electron emission passes through.

By varying the charge on the grid, the current leaving the plate can be varied, as well. A triode may be used to control electric current. But since a triode can also amplify current, a circuit in which triodes both amplify and control current is set up. As weak current is being amplified, a very small change in the charge on the grid can produce a very big change in plate current. This is how an electron tube can delicately and precisely control electric current.

## Triode as Receiver, or Detector

An electron tube can act as a receiver, or detector, of radio (electromagnetic) waves. You will remember that John Ambrose Fleming proved this with his electronic valve. And you may remember, from Heinrich Hertz's experiment, that a receiver changes radio waves to electric current. Furthermore, Reginald Fessenden's work would lead you to think, correctly, that a receiver detecting radio waves produced by an alternating current generator would change these waves back to alternating electric current. Also, as alternating current continually changes its direction, we say it swings back and forth from positive to negative. A diagram of an alternating current wave is shown here.

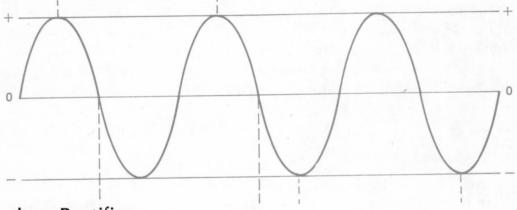

## Triode as Rectifier

Suppose we have a triode acting as a detector, and suppose the only current we send into the electron tube is going to the filament. Incoming radio waves, however, are producing in the plate a current that varies from positive to negative, millions of times a second. Half of the time the plate is charged positive and half of the time negative. This means that half of the time the plate is attracting electrons from the emitter and half of the time it is repelling electrons. Only when the received radio wave generates a positive current, charging the plate positive, will current flow from the plate. By comparing a diagram of that alternating current *(above)*, with the one at the top of the following page, you will see that the bottom half of every wave is cut off. The current that is left no longer alternates; it is a direct current that builds up from zero strength and goes back to zero. Changing alternating current to direct current is called *rectifying;* and the electron tube is a *rectifier*.

Suppose we charge the plate permanently positive, and let the grid do the detecting. Also, we will put a small negative charge on the grid. Now, when the

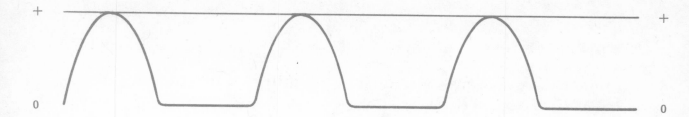

incoming radio wave generates a positive charge in the grid, the grid will be a little less negative, or more positive, and the current that is already flowing to the positively charged plate will be made stronger by the positive part of the incoming wave. When the incoming wave generates a negative charge in the grid, the grid will be even more negative. But since the charge on the grid is weak and the generated charge is even weaker, the grid will not stop the emitted electrons from traveling to the plate; it will simply decrease their number. This means that the direct current leaving the plate will increase and decrease, but never drop to zero. If the strength of the charges on the plate and grid are properly chosen, the rectified current will look like that diagrammed below. In practice, electronic engineers can rectify the current generated by radio waves so that it is almost a straight line, but they use means more complicated than a simple triode.

## Triode as Oscillator

Besides being an amplifier, a detector, and a rectifier, an electron tube can act upon electric current in another way that is very useful to radio broadcasting. An electron tube can be an *oscillator*. This simply means that it can generate alternating current. Instead of using a high-speed electrical generator, as Fessenden did, broadcasting stations generate radio waves by means of electron tubes. If it were not for the electron-tube oscillator, modern broadcasting would be impossible. Some radio waves alternate from positive to negative billions of times a second. It would be impossible to construct an electric generator with an armature that revolves billions—or even millions—of times a second.

## TRANSISTORS

Forty-seven years after the invention of the electron tube, a new device, the *transistor,* appeared in electronics. This device soon took over almost all the jobs that were done by electron tubes. The transistor was invented at the Bell Telephone Laboratories by William Shockley, John Bardeen, and Walter Brattain.

Transistors are very small, compared to electron tubes. The average electron tube is about the size of two marshmallows stacked one on top of the other. Large electron tubes, such as the oscillators in broadcasting stations, may be two feet tall. The smallest electron tubes are the size of a peanut. A large transistor, in comparison, is the size of an eraser on a pencil. The average transistor is about the size of a quarter-inch length cut off a round lollipop stick. In earth satellites, where small size and light weight are all-important, transistors no larger around than the period at the end of this sentence, and as thick as only two sheets of paper, are in operation. Other small transistors are about as long as this letter "i" and no thicker than sewing thread.

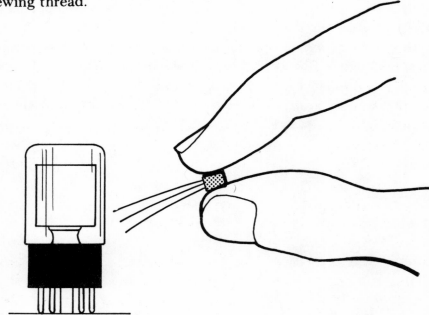

## Semiconductors and Doping

Transistors are made of materials called *semiconductors. Semi* means "partly," so a semiconductor is partly a conductor. In other words, electric current—great numbers of electrons—move through a semiconductor only fairly well. Two substances from which semiconductors can be made are the elements silicon and germanium. When pure, neither of these elements will conduct electricity at all well. However, if a small amount of arsenic is added to pure germanium, the mixture becomes a semiconductor. A small amount of aluminum added to pure silicon will provide the same result. The small amounts of elements which are added are called *impurities.*

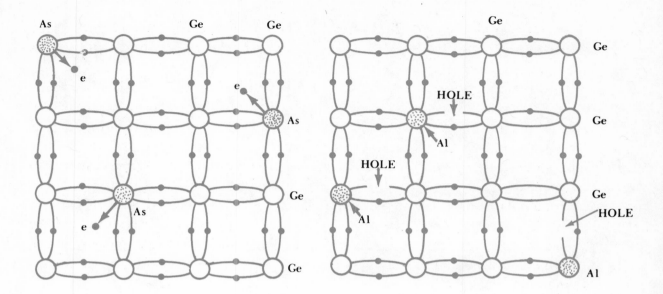

Adding an impurity to an element is called *doping*. Silicon and germanium are made up of small units called *crystals*. The atoms of a crystal are arranged in a regular pattern. If a crystal is doped with arsenic (As) as the impurity *(above, left)*, some arsenic atoms will take the places of silicon or germanium (Ge) atoms and will provide large numbers of electrons (e) not bound to atoms. If a crystal is doped with aluminum (Al), aluminum atoms will take the places of some silicon or germanium atoms. This will cause the crystal to have too few electrons, leaving empty spaces where the electrons should be *(above, right)*. These empty spaces are called holes.

Electrons are, of course, negative electric charges. The holes, then, are positive charges. Both electrons and holes move through semiconductors. To understand how electrons and holes move, think of a theater in which about one-fourth of the seats are empty. No two empty seats are next to each other. The seats in which people are sitting represent electrons. The empty seats represent holes. Now, suppose that all of the people sitting in the front row leave the theater. Then all of the remaining people move forward one row, and new people coming into the theater take seats in the last row. If people continually leave the theater from the front row, and those that are left continue to move forward, and new people always take seats in the last row, it will appear as if both the people and the empty seats are moving—the people going forward, the empty seats moving backward. In the same way, when electrons travel through a semiconductor, they fill holes, but leave new holes in the places from which they moved.

A semiconductor having more moving electrons than holes is called an *n-type* semiconductor. The *n* stands for "negative" and refers to the kind of electrical charge carried by electrons. A semiconductor having more holes than electrons is called a *p-type* semiconductor. The *p* stands for "positive" and refers to the kind of charge carried by the holes.

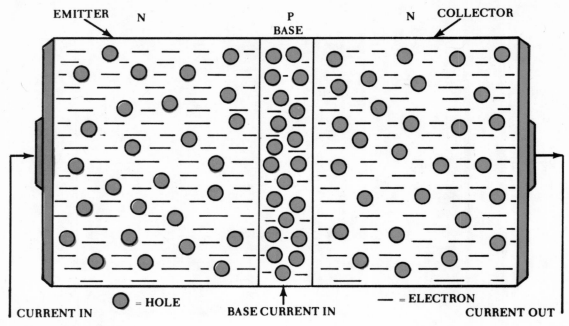

EMITTER    N          P       N    COLLECTOR
BASE

⬤ = HOLE        — = ELECTRON

CURRENT IN           BASE CURRENT IN       CURRENT OUT

## N-p-n Transistor

There are several types of transistors, but the kind that will best show how a transistor works is the *junction transistor*. This transistor is made of a thin slice of semiconductor material of one type sandwiched between two thicker slices of semiconductor material of the other type. For example, an n-p-n junction transistor is made of a middle slice of p-type semiconductor sandwiched between two thicker slices of n-type semiconductor. The "n" slice through which electric current enters the transistor is called the *emitter*. The "n" slice on the side from which current leaves the transistor is the *collector*. Wires are soldered to the end surfaces of both emitter and collector. The middle slice, the "p" slice, is called the *base*, and a wire is soldered to one of its outside surfaces. A surface where semiconductor slices meet is called a *junction*.

An electric current sent into the emitter begins to move electrons toward the base, and holes in the opposite direction. Since the emitter is a slice of n-type semiconductor, there are more electrons moving toward the junction with the base than there are holes moving away. The electron flow lasts only a very short time because the n-p junction blocks the electrons from crossing over to the base. When a small amount of electric current is sent into the base, however, the junction no longer blocks the flow of electrons. Instead, they cross the base to the collector, and leave the transistor through the wire connected to the collector.

Most important, a small increase in the current flowing into the base results in a large increase in the current flowing out of the transistor. In other words, the transistor can amplify current. Also, by increasing and decreasing the amount of current flowing into the base, you can precisely and delicately control the amount of current flowing out of the collector.

You can easily see the similarity between a transistor and a triode electron tube. The transistor's emitter slice of semiconductor material acts like the triode's

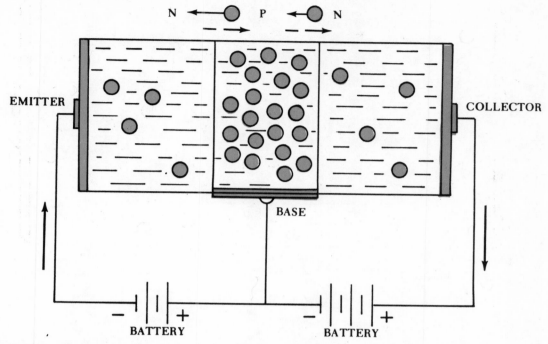

filament-and-sleeve emitter, the cathode. The transistor's base acts like the electron tube's grid. And the transistor's collector acts like the electron tube's plate, the anode. Also, the movement of electrons in the transistor is like electron emission in an electron tube. With all of these features, you can readily understand why transistors have replaced electron tubes in many electronic devices.

It takes time for the filament of an electron tube to become hot enough to cause the cathode to emit enough electrons. But emission of electrons in a transistor begins immediately. Thus, a radio using electron tubes has a warm-up period, but a transistorized radio works immediately upon being turned on. In addition to being smaller than electron tubes, transistors are much more rugged. The delicate filament and grid wires of an electron tube are easily broken; while a transistor, being a tightly joined sandwich of three pieces of solid semiconductor material, is almost unbreakable.

Transistors do have disadvantages, however. They cannot control a large flow of electric current, nor can they amplify radio waves as well as electron tubes. Also, when an electron tube burns out, you can see it easily because the filament does not glow. To find a transistor that has burned out, you need special instruments.

## Diodes

You may have heard radios, televisions, walkie-talkies and other devices described as having a certain number of transistors and a certain number of *diodes*. A diode is like a transistor, but is made of only two slices of semiconductor material. One is a "p" slice, and the other is an "n" slice.

A diode is a one-way door for electric current. It is easy to push electrons across the n-p junction from the "n" half to the "p" half, but not in the opposite direction. Therefore, if alternating current is sent into a diode, when the current is moving in the direction that sends it into the "n" half, the current passes through the diode. When current enters the "p" half, it cannot cross the n-p junction, and so does not pass through and out of the diode. Thus, the diode acts as a rectifier, changing alternating current to direct current.

A diode is photoelectric, generating electricity when light strikes it. One type of diode is used to make solar batteries, which are described in the section on electricity.

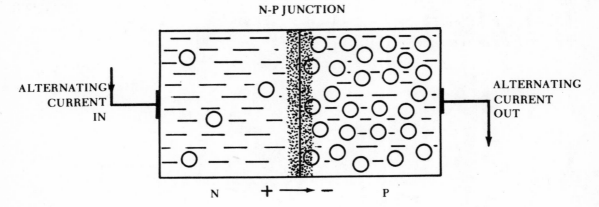

N-P JUNCTION

ALTERNATING CURRENT IN

ALTERNATING CURRENT OUT

N + → − P

# RADIO BROADCASTING AND RECEIVING

We have learned how most of the basic parts of a radio work. Now, let us see how a radio itself works.

In the studio of a broadcasting station, a performer sings or speaks. The sound waves of his voice move through the air to a microphone which works like the transmitter, or mouthpiece, of a telephone. It changes sound waves to electrical impulses. A microphone, though, is far more sensitive; it can pick up sounds of higher and lower pitch. The electrical impulses made by the singer's voice are far too weak to produce electromagnetic waves that could be broadcast very far. So, the impulses go from the microphone to a group of electron tubes that greatly amplify the current.

## Audio Frequency and Radio Frequency

The microphone current is called the *audio frequency* current. "Audio" comes from a Latin word meaning "to hear," and audio frequency refers to the fact that the frequency of the current is the same as the sound waves that enter the microphone. Audio frequency varies from about 100 to 17,000 hertzes. A singer's voice ranges from about 100 to 750 hertzes, so the audio frequency would span this same range. After being amplified, the audio frequency current goes on its way to the broadcasting antenna. The amplitudes of audio frequency impulses vary irregularly, as shown here.

Meanwhile, another group of electron tubes, oscillators, are continually producing a series of alternating-current impulses that range from 300,000 to 3,000,000 hertzes. The impulses vary from plus to minus, and the amplitude of each wave is exactly like all the others. This is the *radio frequency* current.

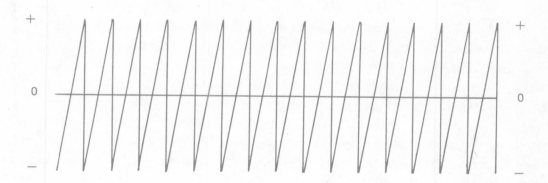

On the way to the broadcasting antenna, this current meets the audio frequency current. The irregular amplitudes of the audio frequency change, or *modulate*, the regular amplitudes of the radio frequency, as shown here.

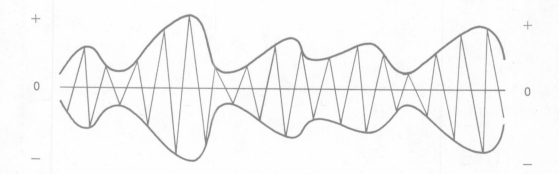

The modulated current goes to the broadcasting antenna, where it produces electromagnetic waves, which are radio waves. The radio frequency current, being much more powerful than the audio frequency, provides the power for broadcasting. Electronic engineers say that radio frequency waves carry the audio frequency; so the radio frequency waves are called *carrier* waves.

## Radio Receiver

A radio receiver traps the broadcast waves by a single wire, an arrangement of several wires, or a metal rod, all of which make up different kinds of *receiving antennae*. The flexible metal rod extending upward from a front fender of an automobile is one kind of receiving antenna with which you are familiar. When radio waves strike the antenna, they are changed to impulses of electric current.

If you have ever tried to listen to the same radio station during a long automobile trip, you know that the farther you travel from the station, the fainter the broadcast becomes. Finally, you are so far away that you cannot receive radio waves from that station any more. The electrical energy in radio waves becomes weaker as the waves travel away from the broadcasting antenna. The average broadcast wave received by a radio has the power of only a few millionths of a watt. The radio must strengthen the very weak current produced by the radio waves. The current impulses must be strong enough to move the diaphragm of a loudspeaker. To make weak impulses strong, they are sent to one or more electron tubes or transistors that amplify the current by any amount from hundreds of thousands to millions of times.

Electrical impulses produced by the received radio waves still have the form shown by the last diagram. The positive amplitudes (above the zero amplitude line) are opposed by the negative amplitudes (below the zero amplitude line); when the amplitude is high on the positive side, it is low on the negative side. If these electrical impulses were sent directly to the loudspeaker, which works very much like the receiver of a telephone, no sound would be produced. While the upper half of the impulse was trying to push the diaphragm of the speaker, the lower half of the impulse would be trying to pull the diaphragm. As a result, the diaphragm would not move. To overcome this problem, the current has to be rectified by means of transistors or electron tubes—the lower half of the impulse is cut off.

The current still is not ready to go to the speaker. We must first eliminate the carrier current (the radio frequency), once it has done its job of carrying the audio frequency from the broadcasting station to the radio receiver. The radio frequency is removed by a group of devices that make up a *filter*. The audio frequency passes through the filter, the radio frequency is held back.

Finally, the current that enters the loudspeaker is exactly like the current produced in the microphone by the sound waves made by the singer's voice. This current moving the diaphragm of the loudspeaker, produces sounds almost exactly like those made by the singer.

As we have seen, the audio frequency modulates the radio-frequency carrier current by changing the amplitude of the radio frequency current. This kind of modulation, then, is called amplitude modulation and is abbreviated AM.

## FREQUENCY MODULATION (FM)

There is another kind of modulation of radio waves. It is called *frequency modulation*, or *FM*. As the name suggests, the frequency of the carrier current is modulated; the amplitude is not changed.

In frequency modulation, when the audio frequency current is positive, the carrier (radio frequency) current is jammed together; when the audio frequency is negative, the radio frequency is spread apart. The frequencies of FM broadcasting are much higher than those of AM. AM frequencies range in the hundreds of thousands of hertzes, while FM ranges in the millions of hertzes.

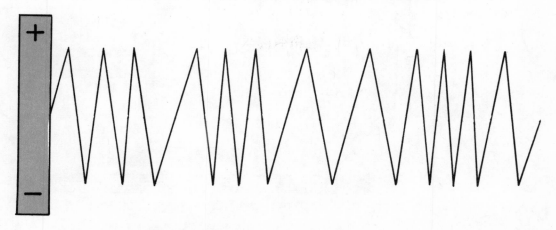

FM is almost entirely free of static. You know static as the scraping and crackling sounds that are frequently heard from a radio. These sounds are made by electromagnetic waves produced and broadcast by moving electrical discharges in automobile spark plugs, electric appliances and other electric machines, and lightning bolts. These waves, trapped by a radio antenna, cause static. Static interferes with AM broadcasting because the amplitude of the waves are modulated by the static waves. Static does not interfere with FM broadcasting because static does nothing to modulate the frequency of radio waves, and FM waves are frequency modulated only.

## TELEVISION

There is much similarity between radio broadcasting and television broadcasting. In radio, sound waves are changed to electromagnetic waves, broadcast, and then changed back to sound waves. In television, light waves (which *are* electromagnetic waves) are changed to waves of lower frequency, broadcast, and then raised again to the frequency of light.

### Image Orthicon

In a studio, when a television camera is focused on an object, light reflected from the object enters the lens of the camera. The lens focuses the light on a metal screen in a large electron tube. In the most common type of television camera, the electron tube is called an *image orthicon*. The metal screen is so thin that light can pass through it as through tissue paper. The metal of which the screen is made is *photoelectric*. This means that when light strikes it, electrons are knocked out of

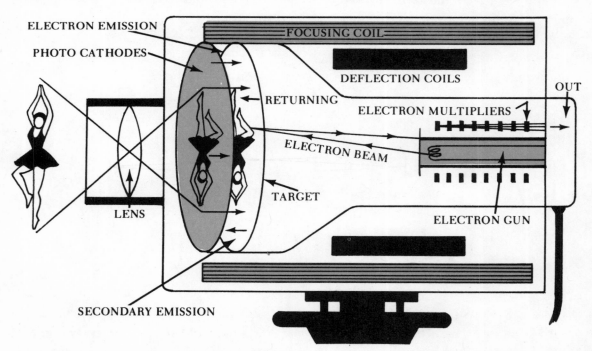

the metal atoms; the brighter the light, the greater the number of electrons that are knocked out of the screen. As the provider of electrons, the screen is the cathode. And the electrons that leave the cathode are a form of electron emission. The emitted electrons strike a metal plate, called the *target*, that is close behind the photoelectric screen. The emitted electrons strike the target in exactly the same pattern as those knocked out of the screen by light that entered the TV camera.

At the back of the image orthicon is an *electron gun,* a device containing an incandescent filament as a cathode which emits electrons. These electrons are sent through a series of very small openings which form an electron beam. The beam is swept across the back of the target by electromagnets, called *deflection coils,* that both repel and attract the electrons, moving the beam back and forth. Where the target has lost electrons it regains them from the beam. Where no electrons were knocked out of the target, the electron beam is repelled. As a result, the electron beam loses electrons in the same pattern as the cathode screen lost them.

The electron beam sweeps over, or *scans,* the target in two successive sweeps. Each sweep begins at the top and zigzags to the bottom. The first downsweep consists of 262 1/2 back-and-forth movements, or lines. The second downsweep covers 262 1/2 alternate lines. Each downsweep takes one-sixtieth of a second, so the entire target is scanned in one-sixtieth of a second.

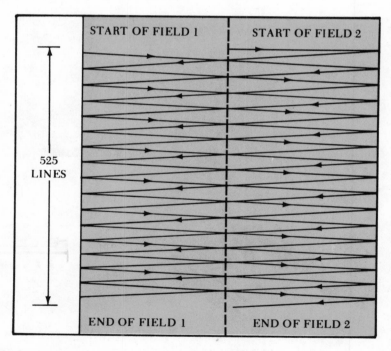

The repelled scanning beam is a kind of electric current. It is the *video frequency,* or *video signal.* Just as the audio frequency current in radio is amplified, so is the video signal. Also as in radio, the video signal is broadcast along with a carrier current. The frequency of the broadcast waves is in the tens of millions of hertzes. And the carrier current is modulated by the video signal.

## Kinescope

A television receiver has, as its main part, a large electron tube called a *kinescope*. It is somewhat like an image orthicon. At the back of the kinescope is an electron gun. At the front is a screen made of a material that lights up momentarily. This screen is the one we look at to see the picture.

Television waves enter a set through a TV antenna. They are changed to current; then they are amplified, rectified and filtered by circuits including electron tubes and transistors. Finally, they arrive at the electron gun, which fires at the screen an electron beam having exactly the same pattern as the one reflected from the target in the image orthicon at the broadcasting station. Wherever an electron strikes the screen, a light patch appears; where electrons are missing, there is a dark patch. Combinations of light and dark patches make up the picture. In making the picture, the electron gun scans the screen at exactly the same rate—30 times a second—as the gun in the television camera. This results in the screen lighting up with exactly the same pattern of light as that which entered the studio television camera. Thus you see on your TV screen the same things the camera "saw" in the studio.

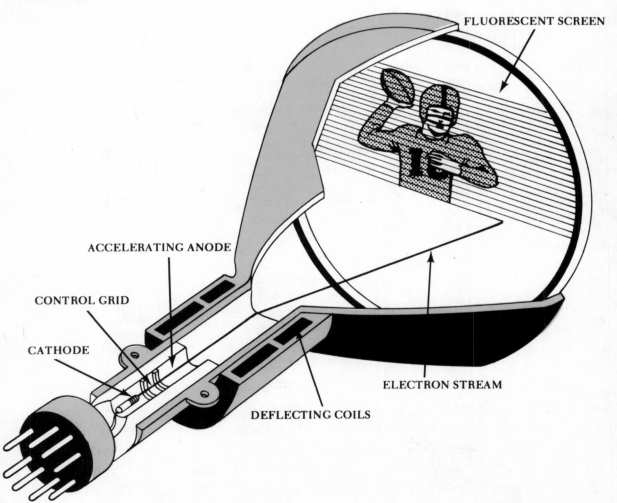

FLUORESCENT SCREEN

ACCELERATING ANODE

CONTROL GRID

CATHODE

DEFLECTING COILS

ELECTRON STREAM

## Color TV

Color television uses three image orthicon tubes. In one, the electron beam is patterned only by red light, a second uses only green light, and a third, only blue light. The video signals from all three cameras go to electronic equipment that combines and uses them to modulate a carrier current. All are broadcast as one series of television waves, which include I, Q, and Y signals. The I and Q signals are the ones produced by the three color cameras picking up the colors of televised objects. Engineers say the I and Q signals "carry the color information." The Y signal carries the brightness information, transmitting the brightness of the light entering the camera.

When the I, Q and Y signals enter a color TV receiver, electronic devices sort out the I and Q signals. These go to the three electron guns in the kinescope, one for each color broadcast. The screen has a special coating that glows red, green, or blue, depending upon which gun is "shooting" its electron beam. It thereby gives the screen almost the same colors "seen" by the television camera. Then the Y signal is mixed with the I and Q signals, giving the colors on the screen the same brightness as the televised scene.

If a color TV broadcast is picked up by the antenna of a receiver that is not equipped to form a color picture, only the Y signal is used. The result is a perfectly good black-and-white picture.

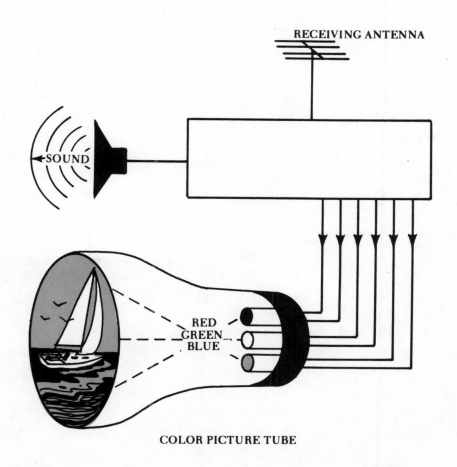

COLOR PICTURE TUBE

# RECORDING SOUND ON FILM

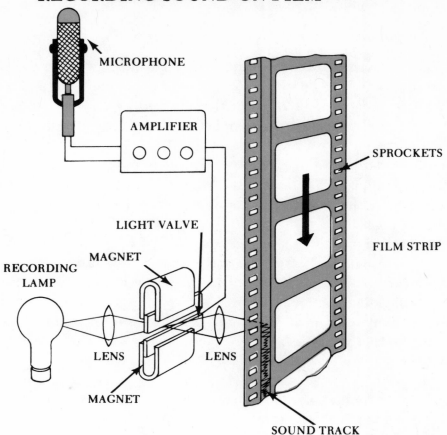

MICROPHONE

AMPLIFIER

LIGHT VALVE

SPROCKETS

FILM STRIP

MAGNET

RECORDING
LAMP

LENS

LENS

MAGNET

SOUND TRACK

## SOUND MOVIES

The earliest movies were silent. When they were shown in a theater, the audience read what the actors were saying as printed words projected on the screen. Years later, the first sound movies used phonograph discs to bring to the audience the sounds of what was happening in the picture. The discs were recorded while the movie was being filmed. When the movie was shown in a theater, the phonograph disc was played and amplified through loudspeakers. Sometimes the disc and film got out of step, and what the actors were saying did not have much to do with what they were doing. Finally, as is done nowadays, sound was recorded electronically on the film alongside the pictures.

In the electronic process, when a film is being made, a microphone picks up the actors' voices and other sounds of the scene the camera is photographing. The microphone changes the sound into electric current of varying strength. This current goes to two electromagnets that open and close a slit between two flat pieces of metal. When the current from the microphone is strong, the electromagnets pull the pieces of metal farther apart, widening the slit. When the current is weak, springs attached to the pieces of metal push them together, narrowing the slit. A beam of light from an electric lamp is directed through the constantly widening and narrowing slit. The light strikes the movie film alongside the light

# PLAYBACK OF SOUND ON FILM

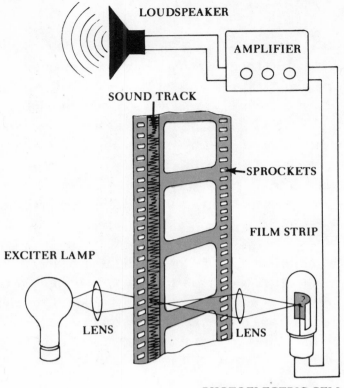

entering the camera lens. When the film is developed, the varying amounts of light that passed through the widening and narrowing slit show up as a row of light and dark areas alongside the pictures. The row is called a *sound track.*

When the film is projected in a theater, a special electric lamp shines a beam through the sound track. This beam falls on an electronic tube called a *photoelectric cell,* or *photocell.* Inside this device is a metal plate coated with another metal that emits electrons when struck by light. This coated plate is the cathode. Another metal plate nearby is the anode. It is kept positively charged, so that any electrons emitted by the cathode will be attracted to the anode. Except for a round window in front of the cathode, the inside of the glass bulb is covered with silver paint that keeps out light. Light entering the window and striking the cathode causes it to emit electrons that stream to the positively charged plate, and an electric current flows out of the photocell.

The beam of light, passing through the sound track on the film, enters the window of the photocell. The brighter the light falling on the cathode, the more electrons it emits, and the larger the current is that flows out of the photocell. The lighter areas of the sound track let more light reach the photocell; the darker areas decrease the brightness of the light beam. The resulting electric current of varying strengths goes to loudspeakers that change the current into sound, just as a telephone receiver does.

# ELECTRON MICROSCOPE

You probably know that a microscope is an instrument that makes it possible to see very small objects, such as bacteria and animals made up of only one cell. Light is needed to make most microscopes work. The light is reflected from, or passes through, the small object you wish to see. Then the light goes into a series of glass lenses that spread the rays, and this magnifies the object. There are some objects, however, that are so small they cannot be seen even with this kind of microscope. Viruses, for example, cannot be seen with a microscope that uses light.

Light is made up of electromagnetic waves. If the object beneath the lenses of the microscope is smaller than the shortest wavelength of light, the light cannot be reflected from the object, nor can it cast a shadow. There is no way for us to see an object this small directly.

Scientists have therefore substituted for the light a beam of electrons. The electrons are much smaller than the shortest wavelength of light. A beam made up of billions of electrons starts as emission from a hot cathode. The electron emission is shaped into a beam by means of a series of magnets that concentrate and direct the electrons in much the same way that glass lenses focus light. The magnets are called magnetic lenses.

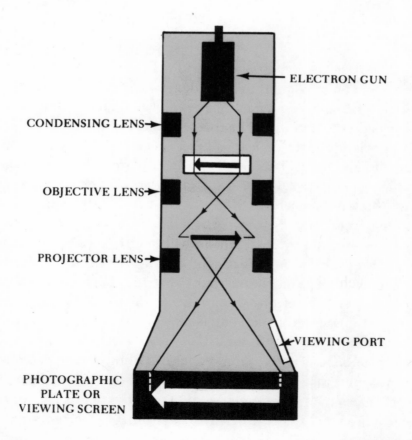

ELECTRON GUN

CONDENSING LENS→

OBJECTIVE LENS→

PROJECTOR LENS→

←VIEWING PORT

PHOTOGRAPHIC
PLATE OR
VIEWING SCREEN

The focused electron beam is directed upon the object to be examined. The electrons either pass through the object or bounce off it. If the electrons pass through, more pass through the thinner parts and fewer through the thicker parts. If the electrons bounce off the object, they cast its shadow. The electron beam acts upon photographic film in almost exactly the same way as a beam of light. This enables us to photograph the object. Also, electrons reflected from the object can be directed upon a screen coated with a fluorescent material, one that gives off light where struck by electrons. Looking at the screen, an electron-microscope operator can see an image of the object being examined. By focusing the electron beam properly, we can magnify objects more than 30,000 times their natural size. Then, by enlarging the photograph made by the electrons, we can further magnify objects to as much as 500,000 times!

The electron microscope has enabled scientists to examine viruses, the smallest known living things, which cause such diseases as chicken pox, measles, mumps, polio, rabies and smallpox. The earliest electron photographs of viruses and other very small particles too often appeared as simply blobs of light and dark. To make the particles stand out clearly, scientists now spray them with vapor of a metal such as gold. The vapor gives the particle a coating of metal only a few atoms thick, but the coating reflects electrons very well. The particle is sprayed from one side. The vapor coats that side of the particle and the area in front, to the sides, and some distance behind. Directly behind the particle, however, there is no coating, because the particle itself blocks the vapor. When the particle is electron-photographed, the coated part stands out as a light area, and the uncoated part is seen as a dark shadow. Metallic vapor coating has helped to reveal much information about viruses.

# ENGINES

An engine is a machine for changing energy into work. For example, the engine under the hood of an automobile changes the energy in gasoline into work that moves the auto. But an automobile engine is also called a motor. Why are two names used for the same thing? What is the difference between a motor and an engine? There really is no clear-cut difference. Whether a piece of machinery that changes energy into work is called an engine or a motor is a matter of custom. For example, an electric motor changes electrical energy into work, yet it is never called an electric engine. Also, some railroad locomotives are powered by diesel engines, yet the same kind of engine (although much smaller) under the hood of a passenger automobile is usually called a diesel motor.

# EXTERNAL COMBUSTION: STEAM ENGINE

A steam engine is based on the fact that steam occupies more than 1,600 times as much space as the water from which it comes. The expansion of water into steam exerts a force. It is this force that is being used when a steam engine performs various kinds of work.

The water to make the steam is heated in a boiler. Any kind of fuel—coal, oil, gas, wood, or coke—may be burned to boil the water. The resulting steam flows through a pipe into the engine itself. Since the fuel is burned outside the engine, a steam engine is called an external combustion engine. "External" means outside, and "combustion" means burning.

## Piston Steam Engine

In a modern piston steam engine, steam from the boiler enters a thick-walled metal chamber called a *steam chest*. There are three holes, or *ports*, in the floor of the steam chest. The center port opens into a pipe, the *steam outlet;* the other two ports, one on either side of the center port, open into another thick-walled metal chamber, the *cylinder*. Moving back and forth across the floor of the steam chest is a rectangular box that has no bottom. This is the *D-slide valve*, which always covers the steam outlet port and alternately covers one of the two inlet ports. *(See illustrations at top of the following page.)* Within the cylinder is a tight-fitting cylindrical plunger, the *piston*.

Steam from the boiler rushing through one of the inlet ports strikes one side of the piston and forces it toward the opposite end of the cylinder. The movement of the piston is called a *stroke*.

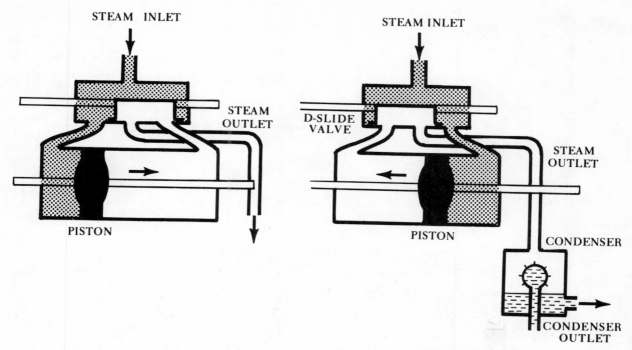

As the piston moves, the D-slide valve also moves so that when the piston reaches the end of its stroke, the port through which the steam entered the cylinder is closed. At the same moment, the D-slide valve opens the other port so that incoming steam is guided to the other side of the piston. Steam striking this side pushes the piston back toward the opposite end of the cylinder.

As the D-slide valve allows steam to enter alternately one intake port and then the other, this valve also keeps open a channel to the steam outlet, where the steam that has just finished pushing the cylinder escapes. The outlet may allow the steam to escape into the air, or it may channel the steam to a chamber called the *condenser*. There the steam is cooled and condenses into water, which may be sent back to the boiler where it is again heated into steam.

The process of entering steam pushing the piston back and forth, the movement of the D-slide valve, and the escape of steam from first one side of the piston and then the other, goes on continually as long as steam enters the steam chest at pressure that is high enough.

A rod, called the *piston rod,* is attached to one side of the piston. The piston rod passes through a steam-tight seal at one end of the cylinder. As the piston moves back and forth, the piston rod moves in and out of the cylinder. The outer end of the rod is attached to a device called a *cross-head,* which moves within a wide metal tube extending outward from the cylinder. The cross-head transmits the movement of the piston to a series of devices that turn a large heavy wheel, the *flywheel.* The back-and-forth motion of the piston is translated into the rotary motion of the flywheel. If the shaft of the flywheel is attached to a machine, the energy in the fuel is finally changed into work performed by the machine.

81

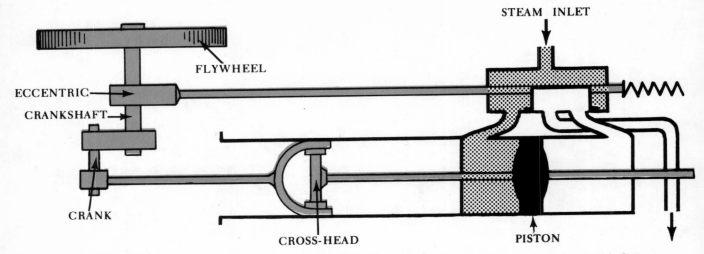

STEAM INLET

FLYWHEEL

ECCENTRIC

CRANKSHAFT

CRANK

CROSS-HEAD

PISTON

Attached to the turning axle of the flywheel is the *eccentric,* a thick metal disc with an off-center hole through which passes the axle of the flywheel. The eccentric translates the rotary motion of the axle into back-and-forth motion. A rod transmits this motion through a steam-tight seal to the D-slide valve inside the steam chest, moving the valve back and forth over the steam ports.

## Steam Turbine

A steam turbine is an engine that contains wheels with rows of curved blades. The wheels are mounted within thick-walled, steam-tight casings.

One type of steam turbine consists of a wheel, called a *rotor,* with a large

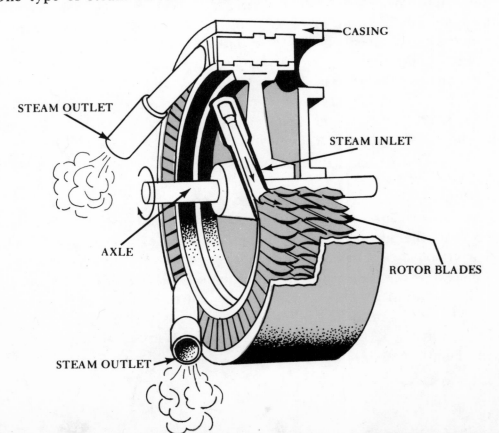

CASING

STEAM OUTLET

STEAM INLET

AXLE

ROTOR BLADES

STEAM OUTLET

number of curved blades that form channels leading from the center of the rotor to nozzles in holes at the rotor's rim. Steam is forced into the channels from the hub of the wheel, and rushes out of the nozzles with such great force that the wheel turns very rapidly. This type of steam engine is called a *reaction turbine*. The reaction of the nozzles to the action of the rapidly escaping steam provides the force that turns the rotor. This is in accord with Newton's Third Law of Motion, which states: "For every action there is an equal and opposite reaction." A simple illustration is that of the man whose jump from a rowboat onto a dock (an action) causes the boat to move away from the dock (the reaction).

A second type of steam turbine has several rotors with curved blades at their rims. The rotors are mounted on a central shaft. Alternating with the rotors and also mounted on the central shaft are rows of metal blades that do not move. These are called *stators*. Steam is forced into the steam-tight casing under very high pressure. It is directed by the stationary blades so as to strike the blades on the rims of the rotors. This causes the rotors and the shaft to spin at a speed of several thousand revolutions per minute. This type of steam engine is called an *impulse turbine*.

## INTERNAL-COMBUSTION ENGINE

An *internal-combustion engine* is one in which the fuel is burned within the engine itself. Upon being burned, the fuel combines with the oxygen of the air and becomes gas. The gas has a volume hundreds of times as great as the fuel from which it came, and the increase in volume takes place in a split second. The expansive force of the hot gas is used to do the work of moving certain parts of the engine.

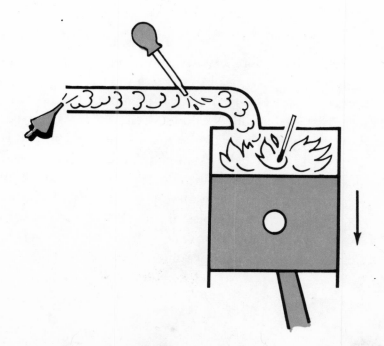

## Gasoline Engine

There are more gasoline-fueled internal-combustion engines than any other kind of engine. All but a very small number of passenger automobiles, all small and medium-sized trucks, and many of the larger trucks are powered by gasoline engines; so are most lawnmowers, tractors and small motorboats, as well as all motorcycles and minibikes. Since this type of engine is so widely used, and since you can easily get to see one, we shall examine its working parts more closely than other types of engines. There are many types of internal-combustion gasoline engines; the type to be described is the one that is used in most automobiles made in the United States and Canada.

The gasoline is stored in the *fuel*, or *gas, tank*, which usually is at the rear of the automobile. A thin pipe, the *fuel line*, runs from the tank to a pump. *(See illustration below.)* This *fuel pump* is needed to make sure that fuel moves from the gas tank, regardless of the position of the car or the direction in which it is moving. A second length of fuel line runs from the pump to the engine.

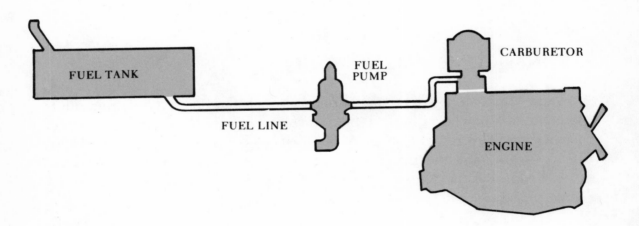

The engine does not burn pure gasoline, but a mixture of gasoline and air. More precisely, what burns is a mixture of gasoline and the oxygen that makes up one-fifth of the volume of air. The air enters the engine through an *air filter*, or *air cleaner*, which consists of a wide flat metal can with holes *(see illustration on following page)* through which air can enter. Inside the can is a thick removable ring made of layers of chemically treated paper put together to form a large number of very small tubes. When air passes through the tubes, most of the dust from the air clings to the paper. This is an important function, because much of the dust in the air consists of small particles of quartz, a material actually harder than the metals of which an automobile engine is made. If dust were not first filtered out, it would act like sandpaper and rapidly wear down the moving parts of the engine.

84

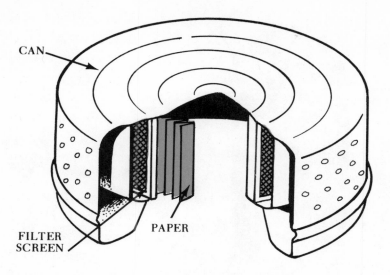

CAN

FILTER
SCREEN

PAPER

A second type of air cleaner, one that is used on most European automobiles, consists of a wide flat can, on the bottom of which is a quarter-inch of oil. Air entering the cleaner is broken up into a stream of small bubbles. The dust in the air bubbles sticks to the oil, allowing clean air to enter the engine.

***Carburetor and Fuel Injection*** • The proper mixture of fuel and air is obtained by means of a *carburetor (see illustration on following page),* which consists of two main parts. One part is the *float chamber,* which is usually about half-full of gasoline and contains a hollow metal can, or *float.* An extension reaching from an upper edge of the float to an opening in the top of the chamber forms the *fuel intake valve.* This valve lets into the chamber more or less gasoline, depending upon the demand of the engine for fuel. When increased demand lessens the amount of gasoline in the float chamber, the float moves downward along with the lowering level of the gasoline. This opens the fuel intake valve, letting into the chamber more gasoline from the gas tank. The incoming gasoline raises the level of the fuel in the float chamber, causing the float to move upward and close the fuel intake valve. Thus, the fuel-operated intake valve works automatically, constantly keeping the amount of fuel in the float chamber at about the same level.

From the float chamber, gasoline goes to the second main part of the carburetor, the *barrel.* This is a thick-walled metal pipe, more than an inch in diameter, in which the mixing of air and fuel takes place. A little more than a third of the distance from the upper end, the inside of the barrel narrows, then tapers back to its original width. A tube having such a shape is called a *venturi.* When air rushes through a venturi, a decrease in air pressure takes place at the narrowest point. At this point is the nozzle opening of a narrow tube that leads upward at a 30-degree angle from the float chamber.

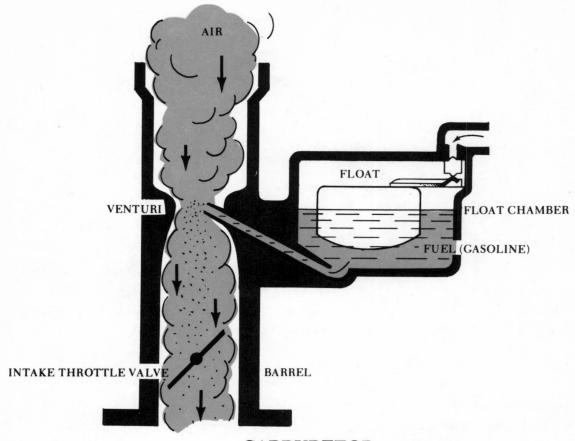

## CARBURETOR

Air that has passed through the air filter rushes into the barrel of the carburetor. At the narrowed part of the venturi, the pressure of the air is decreased. Atmospheric pressure pushes gasoline out of the float chamber, up the narrow tube, and into the stream of air. As a result, the gasoline is broken up into small droplets and mixes with the air. This mixture moves rapidly out the bottom of the carburetor on its way to the cylinders.

The amount of gasoline-and-air mixture passing through the carburetor is increased or decreased by the positioning of a flat disc in the lower part of the venturi tube. The disc is known as the *intake throttle valve*. When the disc is at a right angle to the direction of the flow of the air-fuel mixture, the carburetor is closed, allowing none of the mixture to pass. When the driver of the car pushes down on the accelerator pedal with his foot, he turns the intake throttle so that more of the air-fuel mixture can go through the carburetor. When the driver lets up on the accelerator, a spring automatically turns the throttle valve, so that it is almost closed.

In some types of gasoline engines, fuel and air are mixed without the use of a carburetor. Instead, a system of *fuel injection* is used. In this system, air is forced

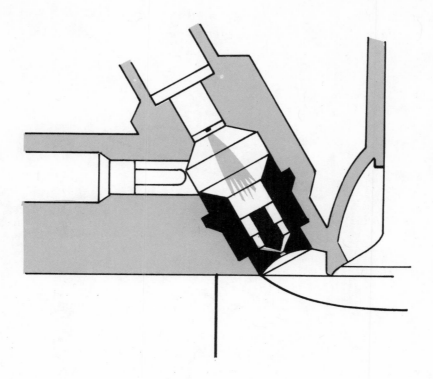

## FUEL INJECTION

into the cylinder (the part of the engine in which the fuel is burned), and then the fuel is squirted, or injected, into the cylinder. The carburetor and the fuel-injection system each has its advantages. Manufacturers of automobiles in the United States use the carburetor in their engines almost exclusively.

On engines that use carburetors, the air-gasoline mixture goes from the lower part of the carburetor to the engine through a wide pipe called the *intake manifold*. The manifold has branching pipes which connect with each cylinder of the engine.

*Cylinders and Pistons* ● The number of cylinders in gasoline engines varies from one to twelve, although sixteen-cylinder engines have been made. One-cylinder engines are found in lawnmowers, minibikes, and some motorcycles. Two-cylinder engines are used in some small automobiles, and in most motorcycles and outboard boat motors. Many types of small European automobiles are powered by four-cylinder engines. Cars made in the United States have six or eight cylinders, and a few have twelve.

The cylinders are holes in a solid metal block, the *engine block*. There are two rows of cylinders, side by side, half the cylinders in one row and half in the other. Six-cylinder engines position the cylinders in upright rows. *(Fig. 1.)* Eight- and twelve-cylinder engines have the rows slanted toward each other at the bottom, making a sort of V. *(Fig. 2.)* Such engines are called V-8's and V-12's.

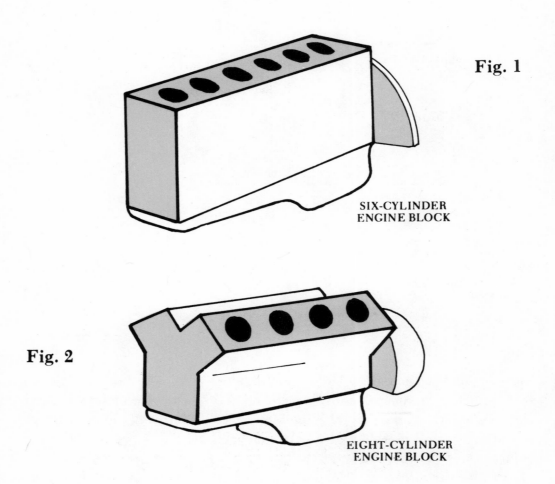

Fig. 1

SIX-CYLINDER
ENGINE BLOCK

Fig. 2

EIGHT-CYLINDER
ENGINE BLOCK

At the top of each cylinder are two openings, in which are placed the valves. *(Fig. 3.)* One valve is an *intake valve*, the other an *exhaust valve*. Also entering an opening at the top of the cylinder is a *spark plug*. Within each cylinder is a *piston*. The upper half of the piston is solid metal; the lower half is hollow. Attached to the inside of a piston, halfway up its length, is a *connecting rod* which transmits the motion of the piston to other parts of the engine. The engine block is covered by a heavy metal block, the *cylinder head (Fig. 4)* which contains hollows that fit over the cylinder valves and spark plugs. The bottom of the engine block is covered by a long, shallow pan called the *oil pan*, which is an oil reservoir.

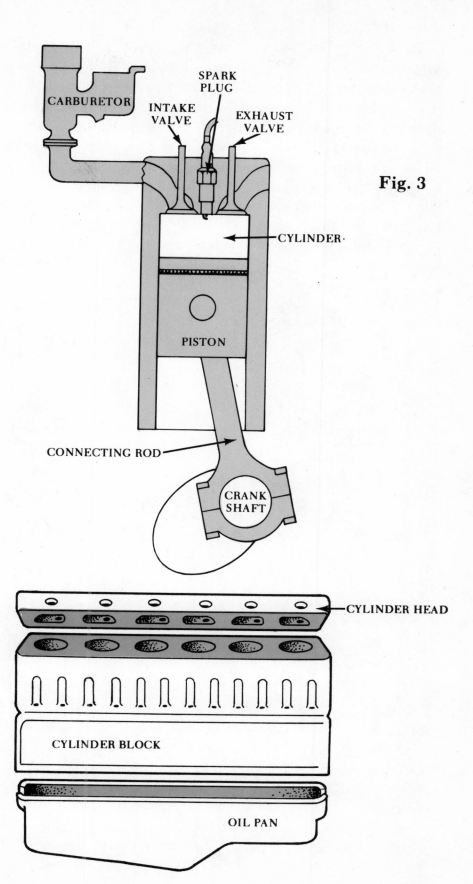

CARBURETOR

SPARK
PLUG

INTAKE
VALVE

EXHAUST
VALVE

Fig. 3

CYLINDER

PISTON

CONNECTING ROD

CRANK
SHAFT

CYLINDER HEAD

Fig. 4

CYLINDER BLOCK

OIL PAN

Almost all gasoline engines work on a cycle of four strokes. *(See illustrations below.)* The strokes are (1) the intake stroke, in which the piston moves away from the valves and the intake valve opens, allowing a mixture of fuel and air to enter the cylinder; (2) the compression stroke, in which the intake valve closes and the piston moves toward the closed valves, compressing the air-fuel mixture; (3) the power stroke, in which the fuel, ignited by a spark supplied by the spark plug, burns very rapidly, or *fires*, and the resulting expanding gases push the piston away from the valves; and (4) the exhaust stroke, in which the exhaust valve opens and the piston, moving toward the open valve, pushes the burned gases out of the cylinder. The exhaust stroke is also called the scavenging stroke. Upon completion of the exhaust stroke, the piston is close to the valves, ready to start another intake stroke.

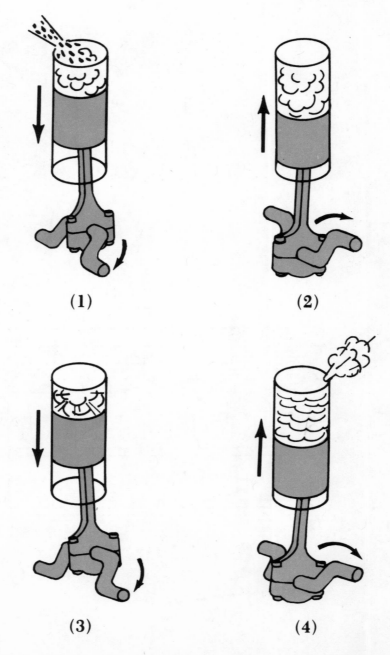

(1)          (2)

(3)          (4)

The exhaust gases are expelled from the engine through the *exhaust manifold,* a branching pipe similar to the intake manifold. From the exhaust manifold the exhaust gases go through the *muffler,* which cuts down the noise of the opening and closing of cylinder valves and the outrush of gases from the cylinder. Finally, the exhaust gases go out of the car and into the atmosphere through the *tailpipe.*

Power generated by the power stroke is transmitted by the connecting rod to the *crankshaft,* a thick zigzag rod of metal. The connections of the rod to the cylinder at the top and the crankshaft at the bottom are like the connections of your leg bone to your knee and ankle. *(See illustrations below.)* And the piston, connecting rod, and crankshaft work as your knee, leg, and ankle do when you are pedaling a bicycle. The crankshaft is housed in a part of the cylinder block called the *upper crankcase.* The lower crankcase is the oil pan.

On each side of the attachment of the connecting rod to the crankshaft is a thick metal disc, or flywheel. Since the flywheel is heavy, it has considerable momentum, and makes the crankshaft turn more smoothly. There are two flywheels for each connecting rod, and so a six-cylinder engine has twelve flywheels.

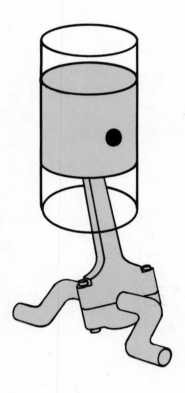
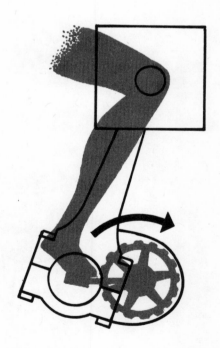

## TRANSMITTAL OF POWER BY
## MECHANICAL AND HUMAN MEANS

*Valves* ● Cylinder valves are called *poppet*, or *mushroom, valves*. In a six-cylinder engine being driven at eighty miles an hour, each cylinder fires two thousand times every minute, or 33 times per second. Since there is an intake stroke and an exhaust stroke for each firing, the intake valve and the exhaust valve must each open and close two thousand times every minute. The opening and closing action is controlled by a *camshaft*, a long, straight metal rod with specially shaped knobs called *cams*. Resting on the cams are short metal cylinders called *valve lifters*. Connected to the valve lifters are *push rods* that go all the way through the engine block to the cylinder head. The upper end of a push rod is connected to one side of a seesaw-like device called a *rocker arm*. The other end of the rocker arm is attached to the end of the poppet valve projecting outside the cylinder. Surrounding the projecting part of the poppet valve is a heavy spring.

The turning camshaft turns the cams which alternately push up and let down the valve lifters and push rods. Each push rod pushes up one side of a rocker arm while the other side of the rocker arm pushes down a poppet valve. This uncovers the opening into the cylinder for either exhaust or intake, depending on which valve it is.

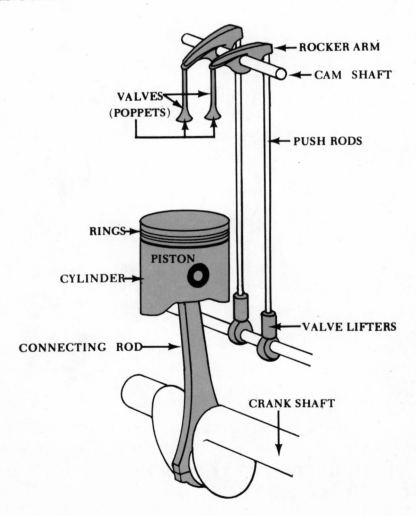

The timing of the opening and closing of the valves is extremely important. If, for example, the intake valve did not entirely close during the first half of the compression stroke, half the fuel-air mixture would be pushed back into the carburetor and the remaining half would not produce the needed power when burned. Precise timing of valve actions is controlled by *timing gears* connected to both the crankshaft and the camshaft.

Proper mixing of the air and fuel, proper timing of valve actions, and the movements of the other parts of the engine would be useless if the air-fuel mixture did not burn properly. The air-fuel mixture is, as we have seen, ignited by a spark produced by a spark plug. This is a spark plug:

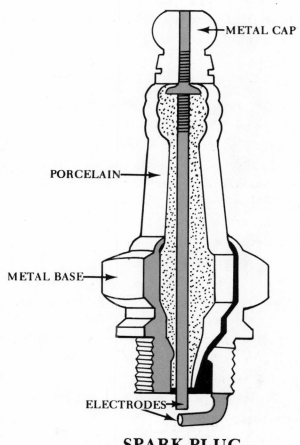

METAL CAP

PORCELAIN

METAL BASE

ELECTRODES

## SPARK PLUG

*Spark Plugs* ● A spark plug consists of a metal base, or shell, that surrounds the lower part of a cylinder made of porcelain or some other material that insulates against the passage of electricity. At the top of the insulating cylinder is a metal cap, and running down from the cap through the insulating cylinder is a thick wire. The bottom of this wire protrudes from the base of the spark plug. This wire is called an *electrode*. Another electrode, a short L-shaped wire, extends downward and inward from the metal shell. The ends of the two electrodes are only a few hundredths of an inch apart. Current from the automobile's electrical system enters the center electrode and jumps to the other one. The jumping electric current is in the form of a spark. The appearance of the spark must be timed just right—just at the split-second in which the air-gasoline mixture is compressed against the top of the cylinder by the rising piston. In a six-cylinder automobile moving at eighty miles an hour, a spark plug must produce two thousand perfectly timed sparks each minute. The average spark plug works well through 10,000 to 12,000 miles of driving, during which it ignites 15,000,000 to 18,000,000 cylinderfuls of gasoline-air mixture, and usually does this without a miss.

All of the cylinders of an internal-combustion engine do not fire at once, because no two are in exactly the same part of a stroke at the same time. The crankshaft, as a result, receives a continuous series of pushes from the cylinders which are firing in carefully timed order. Part of this timing depends on proper timing of valve action, which we have discussed. It also depends on the timing of the ignition of the air-gasoline mixture. This timing is controlled by the *ignition system*.

*Ignition System* ● It is the job of the ignition system to deliver a hot powerful spark to each cylinder at exactly the moment when the piston is at the highest point of its compression stroke. The spark begins in a *storage battery*, the automobile's reservoir of electrical energy. Batteries used in cars deliver electric current at six or twelve volts. We may consider a volt to be a measure of the pressure with which a battery pushes out electric current. But six or twelve volts is far too weak to produce a spark with the needed power, so the voltage is increased, or stepped up, by means of an *ignition coil*. This coil really consists of two coils. One coil, the primary, is made up of a few hundred turns of fairly thick wire; the other coil, the secondary, is made up of as many as 25,000 turns of fine wire.

When current flows steadily in the primary coil, nothing happens in the secondary. But when current flow is interrupted, a very high voltage—18,000 to 20,000 volts—is produced in the secondary for a very short time. A device is needed that will break the current in the primary circuit and send a strong surge of current to each spark plug in proper order and timing. This device is a *breaker*. In the center of the breaker is a revolving cam, which has as many points as the engine has cylinders. The cam shown in the illustration is for a six-cylinder engine. The points on the cam strike a spring-loaded arm that is one of a pair of contacts. The cam is turned by a rod that is geared to the camshaft. As each point of the revolving cam strikes the breaker arm, the contacts open; then the spring closes them. The contacts remain closed less than one-hundredth of a second. In that short time, current flows to the primary of the ignition coil. To make sure that the break in the current is clean and that the surge of current between the contact points is strong, a *condenser* (or *capacitor*) is placed in the breaker. The condenser stores electric current; then, when it has stored a certain amount, it releases it all at once. This results in a sudden, sharp, strong spurt of current.

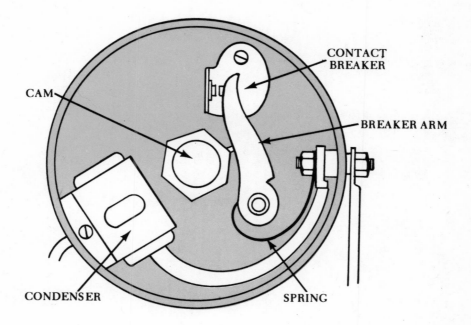

CAM

CONTACT BREAKER

BREAKER ARM

CONDENSER

SPRING

The strong spurt of current produced by the secondary of the ignition coil goes through a rubber-covered wire to a *distributor*. This device sends the current to the spark plugs in the order in which the cylinders are to fire. Within the distributor is a ring of contact points over which a revolving arm slides. The number of contact points is equal to the number of cylinders. You might think of the contact points as the numerals on the dial of a watch and the revolving arm as the minute hand. The distributor is covered by a domed cap. The wire from the ignition coil enters the center of the cap. Thick rubber-covered wires run from the outer part of the distributor cap to the spark plugs, one wire to each plug. As the revolving arm passes over a contact point in the distributor, a spurt of current flows through the wire to the spark plug, making a strong, powerful spark.

## Diesel Engine

Most passenger buses (except for school buses) and the tractors of tractor-trailer trucks are powered by diesel engines. So are many pleasure boats, most ferries, and some other boats. In the United States, steam railroad locomotives have been replaced by diesel locomotives.

A diesel engine is an internal-combustion engine in which fuel is ignited by being sprayed into very hot air. Fuel used in a diesel engine is a special kind of oil.

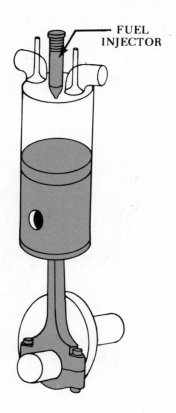

FUEL INJECTOR

A four-stroke diesel engine is much like a gasoline engine minus spark plugs (*see illustration above*). In place of the spark plug there is a fuel injector. On the first stroke, the intake valve opens, and air, rather than an air-fuel mixture, is drawn into the cylinder. The second stroke is a compression stroke in which the air is compressed to one-sixteenth of its original volume—about half the volume to which the air-fuel mixture is compressed in a gasoline engine. Compression heats the air in the diesel engine cylinder to about 1,100° F. Just before compression is complete, the injector squirts fuel into the hot air. The air-fuel mixture burns, expands greatly, and pushes on the piston in a power stroke. On the fourth stroke, the exhaust valve opens and the piston moves toward the valve, expelling the exhaust gases.

Since the air and fuel are mixed in the cylinder, a diesel engine has no carburetor. Also, since there is no spark plug, a diesel engine has no need for a storage battery or an ignition system.

The intake and exhaust valves and the fuel injector are operated by a camshaft; so are the other devices used to open and close valves in a gasoline engine.

In a four-stroke engine, the intake and exhaust strokes are wasted, as far as producing power is concerned. Thus, by eliminating these two strokes, it is possible to have one power stroke for every two strokes of the piston. This is the basis of the improved two-stroke diesel engine.

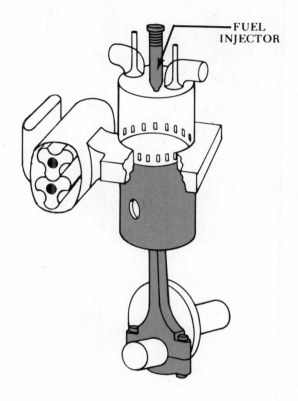

FUEL
INJECTOR

In this engine *(above)*, the two valves are both exhaust valves. The fuel injector is located in the same place as in a four-stroke diesel. An air chamber surrounds the cylinder, and a ring of holes, or *ports*, in the cylinder wall connects with the air chamber. During the intake and exhaust strokes of a four-stroke engine, the piston acts as a pump. In the two-stroke diesel, a pump, or blower, is added and connects with the air chamber.

In the first stroke of a two-stroke engine, the piston is at the bottom of the cylinder, just beginning to move up. *(See illustration, top of following page.)* Both valves are open. The blower is pushing air into the cylinder and the air is pushing the exhaust gases out through the valves. When the top of the rising piston reaches the intake ports, it blocks them, cutting off the intake of air. *(See illustration, bottom of following page.)* As the piston continues upward, the valves close, and the piston compresses the air inside the cylinder. The fuel injector squirts fuel into the hot, compressed air, which fires. The piston is pushed down in the second stroke—the power stroke. When the top of the piston passes the air-intake ports, they are left open. Air from the air chamber rushes in and begins to push out the exhaust gases while the piston finishes its downward movement.

Since a two-stroke diesel fires once for every two strokes, instead of once for every four, it produces twice as much power as a four-stroke engine.

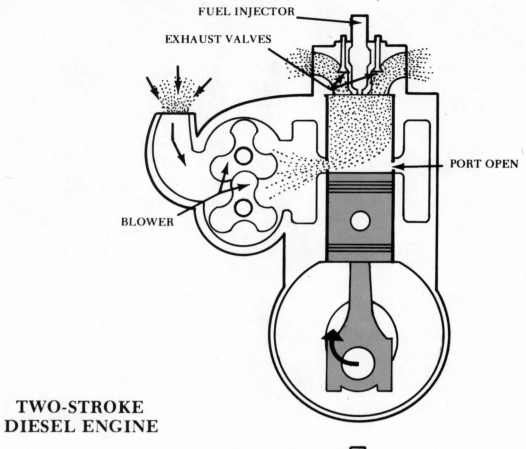

FUEL INJECTOR

EXHAUST VALVES

PORT OPEN

BLOWER

**TWO-STROKE
DIESEL ENGINE**

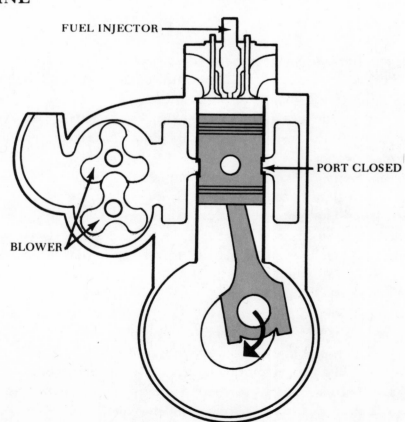

FUEL INJECTOR

PORT CLOSED

BLOWER

## Internal-Combustion, or Gas, Turbines (Jet Engines)

An internal-combustion turbine is similar to an impulse steam turbine. The main difference is that hot gas, instead of steam, turns the turbine rotor. The best-known type of gas turbine is the one used to power aircraft—the jet engine.

The outer part of a jet engine is a metal casing, or housing, open at both ends. Running down the center of the housing is a strong metal shaft. Attached to the shaft at the front end of the engine are bladed wheels, the rotors, revolving between stationary blades, the stators. This arrangement of moving and stationary blades makes up the *compressor*. Air enters the engine at the front, and the compressor rotors, turning at about 11,000 revolutions per minute, squeeze the air, forcing it into eight to twelve *combustion chambers*. These are tubes arranged in a circle around the engine, behind the compressor. The tubes have a large number of holes through which the compressed air enters the combustion chambers. Fuel is pumped through nozzles which squirt it as a spray into each chamber, where it is ignited. Ignition is caused by *ignitor plugs*, which work much like spark plugs in an automobile engine. The ignited fuel burns continuously, so the ignitor plugs are needed only to start the burning. Only two ignitor plugs are needed for all the combustion chambers. The chambers are interconnected by tubes, so that when burning starts in one chamber, it spreads immediately to all the others.

The burning fuel becomes a gas with a volume hundreds of times as great as that of the fuel. Only part of the air entering the compressor is burned in the combustion chambers. The rest is heated by the burning fuel and expands. The expansion of the fuel gases and the heated air causes tremendous pressure within

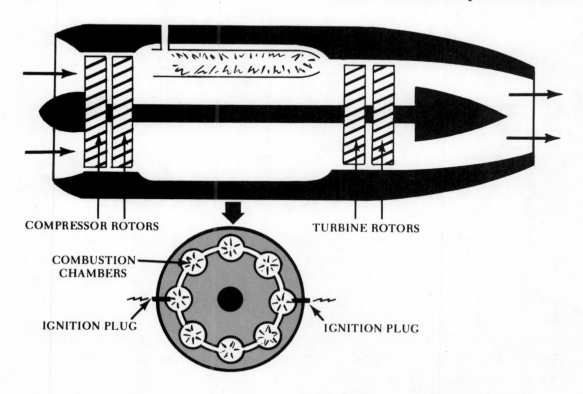

COMPRESSOR ROTORS       TURBINE ROTORS

COMBUSTION CHAMBERS

IGNITION PLUG       IGNITION PLUG

the fuel chamber, and the mixture of exhaust gas and hot air escapes at the rear of the combustion chamber at high speed. Leaving the chamber, the gaseous mixture passes through a turbine. It strikes the blades of the turbine rotor, making the rotor spin very fast.

The turbine and compressor rotors are both fastened securely to the central shaft and therefore rotate at the same speed. The energy for turning the turbine comes from the burning fuel, and the whole object of having an internal-combustion turbine in a jet engine is to turn the rotors of the compressor.

The principle upon which the jet engine is based is summed up in Newton's Third Law of Motion: For every action there is an equal and opposite reaction. Another example of how this principle works: When a gun is fired, it moves backward—"kicks"—with the same force as that with which the bullet moves forward. In a jet engine, the hot gases and air rush out of the rear of the engine casing, providing the action. As a reaction, the engine moves forward. If one or more engines are attached to an airplane, the airplane moves forward with the same force as the torrent of air and gas which moves backward.

If we return to the earlier illustration of the man and the rowboat, a heavy man will put more force into his jump to the dock than a light man. As a result, more force will go into moving the rowboat in the opposite direction. Also, if the man jumps faster, he will have to put more force into his jump; and more force will go into moving the rowboat. If the man is heavy and jumps fast as well, still more force will be expended, and still more force will go into moving the rowboat.

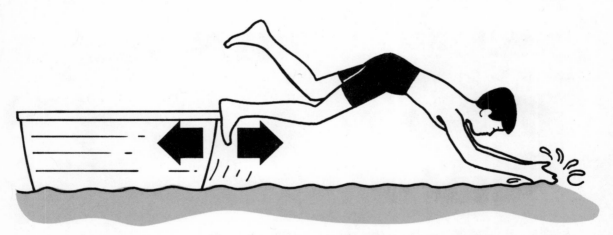

The greater the mass of air and exhaust gas that is pushed out of the rear of a jet engine, the greater will be the force with which the engine moves forward. This fact explains why the compressor forces more air into the engine than is needed to burn the fuel: more air "in" means more air "out" and more force used to push it out.

Also, the faster the mass of gas and air moves out of the engine, the greater the force used to move it out. This is why the air is heated; heating expands the air, and its expansion greatly increases the speed with which it rushes out of the engine. A further increase in speed is obtained by narrowing the rear of the engine housing, the tailpipe.

It is very important to understand that a jet turbine engine does *not* move forward because the air shooting out of the tailpipe pushes on the air behind. What moves the engine forward is the *reaction* to the rearward *action* of the hot air and gases.

## Rocket Engine

Since a jet engine needs air to burn its fuel and provide a heavy mass to push out the rear, a jet engine cannot operate in outer space where there is no air. For travel in outer space, an engine is needed that can work without air. The rocket engine, an internal-combustion reaction engine, fills this need.

A rocket engine consists of stored fuel, one or more combustion chambers, and one or more exhaust nozzles, all housed in a straight tube open at one end. The fuel provides its own oxygen, and therefore can burn without the presence of air. The burning fuel provides gas that rushes out of the open end of the rocket. The reaction to the action of the outrushing gas propels the rocket in the direction opposite to that in which the gas is moving.

*Propellants* • Since a rocket is propelled by gases that result from burning fuel, rocket fuels are called *propellants*. Rocket propellants are of two types, solid and liquid. Solid propellants include black gunpowder, smokeless gunpowder, and other chemical substances such as specially prepared waxes, asphalts, resins, and rubbers.

A solid propellant is simpler to use than a liquid. A solid-propellant rocket engine need only consist of a combustion chamber, an exhaust nozzle, and a device to ignite the propellant.

In a solid-propellant rocket, the fuel is in the form of one or more solid pieces, each of which is called a *grain*. One or more grains together in the rocket's casing, or *skin*, make up the *charge*.

The charge may have one of several shapes. In a small rocket it may fill the entire casing and burn only at its rear. This is an end-burning charge which produces a steady force, or thrust, for a long duration. Or, a channel may run through the length of a charge, resulting in a center-burning charge that burns along its inside surface. This arrangement produces more gas in a shorter time, providing greater rocket thrust. A star-shaped channel provides even more thrust.

## VARIOUS SHAPES OF
## SOLID-PROPELLANT ROCKET CHARGES

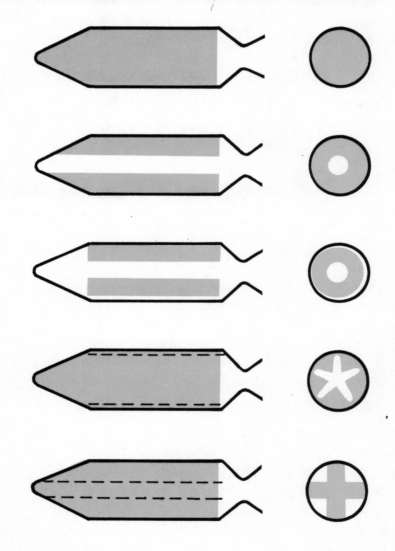

If the pierced charge is separated from the skin, it can then burn on the inside, outside, and end surfaces, all at the same time. This arrangement not only increases thrust, but induces a steady rate of burning. As the charge burns, its outside surfaces become smaller at the same rate its inside surface becomes larger. A charge formed in the shape of a cross also provides quick, even burning.

To start a solid-propellant charge burning, an igniter called a *squib* is used. The squib consists of a container filled with black gunpowder, from which wires extend to contacts for igniting the powder electrically. The squib is placed within, or in contact with, the charge. When the firing button is pushed, the contacts close, and electric current heats the wires rapidly to a very high temperature. The red-hot wires ignite the gunpowder, which in turn ignites the rocket charge. The gas produced by the burning charge blows the remains of the squib and wires out the rear of the rocket.

Another way to ignite a solid propellant is to spray into the charge a liquid which ignites chemically when it comes into contact with the charge. A chemical reaction of this type is called *spontaneous combustion*.

Sometimes liquid-propellant rocket engines carry only one liquid propellant. One such propellant is hydrogen peroxide, the same chemical used as a household antiseptic. If a small amount of another chemical, potassium permanganate, is added to hydrogen peroxide in a combustion chamber, the peroxide decomposes into oxygen and steam, which rush out the rocket's nozzle. A hydrogen peroxide rocket has only a low thrust, but in some situations that is exactly what is wanted. For example, when astronauts want to roll, turn, or dip a space capsule, a low-thrust rocket is just right.

Most liquid-propellant rockets are *bipropellant*, which means that they use two separate liquid propellants. One liquid is called the *fuel;* the other liquid, which usually supplies the oxygen needed for burning, is the *oxidizer*. Alcohol, gasoline, kerosene, and ammonia are among the liquids that are used for rocket fuels. Aniline, hydrazine, and hydrogen are other substances used to fuel rockets. Liquid oxygen, called *LOX*, red fuming nitric acid, and nitrogen tetroxide are oxidizers. LOX is the one most commonly used. The Apollo program's Saturn V booster rockets oxidize hydrogen with LOX.

**Combustion** ● There are two ways to move the fuel and the oxidizer from their separate storage tanks to the combustion chamber: by gas pressure and by pumping. For smaller, short-burning rockets, gas pressure is better. A tank of nonburnable gas under high pressure is connected by pipes to the propellant storage tanks. The pressure of the gas forces the liquids into the combustion chamber. *(See illustration at top of following page.)*

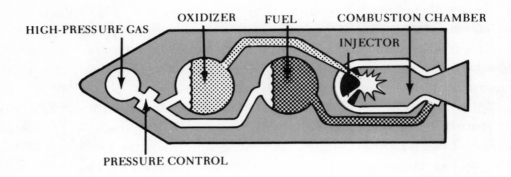

HIGH-PRESSURE GAS      OXIDIZER    FUEL     COMBUSTION CHAMBER

INJECTOR

PRESSURE CONTROL

Unfortunately, this extremely simple gas-pressure system cannot be used with the larger rocket engines. The Saturn V rocket burns 5,700 pounds of kerosene and LOX each second. Pumps are needed to move the propellants to the combustion chamber of such a large rocket. They are called *turbopumps*, because they are driven by gas turbines which either burn the rocket's propellants or have their own fuel supply.

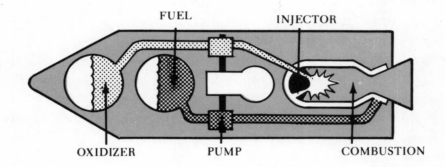

FUEL      INJECTOR

OXIDIZER      PUMP      COMBUSTION

The fuel must be burned in the most efficient manner possible. The fuel and oxidizer must be mixed thoroughly, and the amount of propellants that enters the combustion chamber must be regulated carefully. This task is performed by the *injector,* a device that performs in a rocket somewhat the way the carburetor does in an automobile. The carburetor vaporizes gasoline (fuel), mixes it with air (oxidizer), and sends the mixture to the cylinder (combustion chamber). In one type of injector, the pipes leading from the pumps to the combustion chamber end in a metal cap with thousands of holes, like a shower head. The caps are positioned so that streams of fuel and oxidizer intersect. As the intersecting streams strike each other, the propellants vaporize. The vaporized propellant mixture is immediately ignited.

*Nozzles* ● As in the jet engine, the forward force, or thrust, of a rocket depends on two things: the amount of hot gases rushing out the rear and the velocity with which they move. To increase the amount of gases rushing out of the rear of a rocket, the number of separate rocket engines within the skin is increased. Each engine has one or more exhaust nozzles of its own. The construction of the nozzles plays an important part in determining how fast the gases will shoot out of the rear of the rocket.

A mere hole in the rear of the rocket will produce some thrust, but not very much. Engineers have found that they can improve on the simple hole by adding a cone-shaped nozzle to the outside of the hole. This type of nozzle is called a *divergent* (moving-apart) *nozzle*. Further research has shown that higher exhaust velocity can be obtained from a *convergent* (coming-together) *nozzle*. Gases escaping through this type of nozzle can reach the speed of sound. If a divergent nozzle is added to the outer end of a convergent nozzle, the gases can be accelerated to *supersonic* (faster-than-sound) speeds.

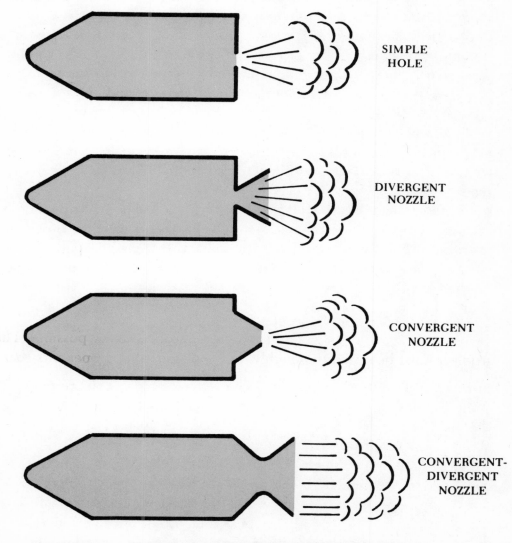

SIMPLE HOLE

DIVERGENT NOZZLE

CONVERGENT NOZZLE

CONVERGENT-DIVERGENT NOZZLE

**VARIOUS SHAPES OF ROCKET NOZZLES**

# COLD AND HEAT

## REFRIGERATOR

A refrigerator is a container for keeping food and other materials cool or cold. The container may be a large room or a boxlike piece of furniture such as that found in most kitchens. The part of the container in which the material is kept cool is called the *refrigeration chamber*. The low temperature within this chamber is produced by a cooling mechanism powered by electricity or gas. The walls and door of the refrigeration chamber are well insulated against the passage of heat through them. This keeps the air and the other contents of the chamber cool for a fairly long time after the cooling machinery has stopped running.

The principles upon which a refrigerating mechanism work are three: (1) evaporation is a cooling process; (2) an evaporating liquid absorbs heat from its surroundings; (3) condensing a vapor to a liquid releases to its surroundings the same amount of heat as that required to evaporate the liquid.

The mechanism of a refrigerator consists of an *evaporator*, a *compressor*, and a *condenser*. The first of these devices is inside the refrigeration chamber, the other two are outside. All three are connected by pipes to form a circuit. Part of this circuit is filled with a liquid called a *refrigerant*, and the rest with the vapor (gaseous state) of this liquid. The refrigerant must be one which will easily vaporize when under low pressure to a liquid and which can be returned to a liquid at ordinary temperatures by compressing the vapor. Some refrigerants are ammonia, carbon dioxide, sulfur dioxide, methyl chloride, and a group known by the trade name Freon.

To understand how a refrigerator works, a kitchen refrigerator will be our example. Food put into the refrigeration chamber is usually at room temperature or warmer. The air in the refrigeration chamber is cool, usually between 36° and 40° F. This air absorbs heat from the food, cooling the food and becoming warm. At the top of the refrigeration chamber is the freezing compartment, surrounded by a zigzag channel of metal tubing within thin metal walls. Or else the whole top of the chamber may be the bottom of the freezer, with a zigzag of metal tubing projecting from the freezer into the chamber. The walls and channel make up the evaporator. Within the evaporator is a partial vacuum which causes the refrigerant to boil and therefore evaporate. The evaporation cools the refrigerant, which in turn absorbs heat from the metal walls. The walls have been absorbing heat from the air that previously absorbed heat from the food. The air is cooled and can absorb more heat from the food.

By the time the refrigerant has circulated through the evaporator to the opposite end from where it entered, the vapor has been warmed by the heat it absorbed. The warm vapor goes through a pipe to the compressor, which is outside the refrigeration chamber and usually near the bottom of the refrigerator. The action of the compressor puts the refrigerant vapor under pressure. The compressed refrigerant vapor goes to a series of metal coils that make up the condenser. The heat from the warm vapor passes through the walls of the coils, warming the surrounding air, which is blown away by an electric fan. (If you hold your hand in front of the grate which is usually below the door of a kitchen refrigerator, you can feel the warm air flowing out.) By losing heat, the compressed refrigerant vapor is cooled, and the cooling condenses it to a liquid.

Because of the action of the compressor, the liquid refrigerant in the condenser is under pressure. The compressed liquid goes through a pipe to the evaporator. The refrigerant enters the evaporator through a very narrow metal tube called a *capillary*, which may or may not be coiled. Also, because of the action of the compressor, the evaporator is kept at a very low pressure. The compressed refrigerant escaping from the narrow metal tubing expands rapidly and, as we have learned, boils.

The cycle of evaporation and condensation of the refrigerant goes on and on—for as long as the compressor is running.

In refrigerators operated by a gas flame, the refrigerant vapor is generated by heating a solution of the refrigerant in water. The vapor is then cooled by running water and is collected in a condenser under sufficient pressure to cause it to liquefy. The liquid refrigerant is then allowed to expand and evaporate in an evaporator.

Inside the refrigeration chamber is a thermostat. When the chamber has been cooled to the desired temperature, the thermostat shuts off the compressor motor. When the chamber becomes too warm—as when warm things are put into the refrigerator or when the door has been open—the thermostat turns the compressor on. In a gas refrigerator the thermostat turns the gas flame up and down.

## FREEZER

A freezer is simply a large insulated container surrounded by the walls of an evaporator. Ice cubes can be made in a freezer, and frozen foods stored in it, because the temperature inside a freezer is about 15° F., which is well below the freezing temperature of water. A freezer is colder than a refrigerator because the freezing chamber is surrounded on all sides by the evaporating refrigerant; however, it is based on the same principle and has the same mechanical parts.

## FROZEN FOOD

Food can be preserved by freezing it. Frozen food does not spoil, or decay. Decay is caused by certain kinds of bacteria and fungi feeding and multiplying in food. These bacteria and fungi cannot feed and multiply when they are frozen, so food does not decay as long as it remains frozen.

Food must be frozen quickly. With a few exceptions, such as salt, sugar, some seasonings, and liquids, food is composed of cells that once made up a living plant or animal. All such cells contain water as the main part of their juices. If plant or animal cells are frozen slowly, large crystals of ice form inside the cells and burst the cell membranes or cell walls. Food frozen slowly is preserved from decay, but when it is thawed for cooking or eating, the ice crystals melt and all the juices flow out, leaving a soggy mass of cell walls or membranes. If, however, food is frozen quickly, the ice crystals that form within the cells are small and do not burst them. When quick-frozen food is thawed, the juices remain in the cells, and the food is almost exactly the same as when it was harvested or butchered.

Foods are frozen commercially by any of three methods:

(1) *Plate freezing.* The food is placed in contact with metal plates that have been cooled to at least 20° below zero Fahrenheit.

(2) *Blast freezing.* The food is placed in an insulated chamber, and a blast of air cooled below minus 20° F. is blown over the food at a speed of several thousand feet a minute.

(3) *Immersion freezing.* The food is immersed in brine or some other liquid that is maintained at a temperature of minus 20° to minus 40° F.

In all these methods, the low temperatures are obtained by the use of refrigeration equipment that works on the same principles as a kitchen refrigerator, but is much larger and far more complex.

Since freezing does not kill the bacteria and fungi that cause decay, frozen food should be eaten soon after thawing, and it should not be kept in the refrigerator for a very long time.

## AIR CONDITIONING

When we speak of air conditioning, we usually mean the cooling of air in buildings during hot weather. When an air-conditioning engineer thinks of his work, he includes the warming of air during cold weather, the control of the humidity and circulation of the air, and the removal of dust from the air.

A cooling air conditioner works on the same principles and has almost the same mechanical parts as a refrigerator. Since an air conditioner must cool a much larger volume of air than is found in the freezing chamber of a refrigerator, the parts of an air conditioner are larger.

## Room Air Conditioner

A room air condifioner is the kind that is placed in a window. It cannot cool much more than the amount of air found in a single medium-sized room. The interior of the air conditioner is divided in two by a thin metal partition. One section projects from the windowsill into the room, while the other projects outside.

The compartment inside the room contains the evaporator with its cooling coils. A small electric fan blows the cooled air into the room through a discharge grill which may be either at the top or the front of the compartment. Replacing the air blown out, air from the room moves through a grill and a dust filter into the compartment. This air is cooled by circulating through the cooling coils; then it is blown back into the room. Since cool air cannot hold as much moisture as warm air, some of the moisture condenses out of the air moving in contact with the cooling coils. Water removed from the air forms drops on the coils which then drip into a pan at the bottom of the air conditioner. This water runs through openings in the bottom of the partition and collects in a pool near the outer end of the air conditioner.

The compartment outside the building contains the compressor and the condenser. A large electric fan, the *condenser fan*, is surrounded by a tubular ring, called the *slinger ring*. This ring is split all around its circumference, and the

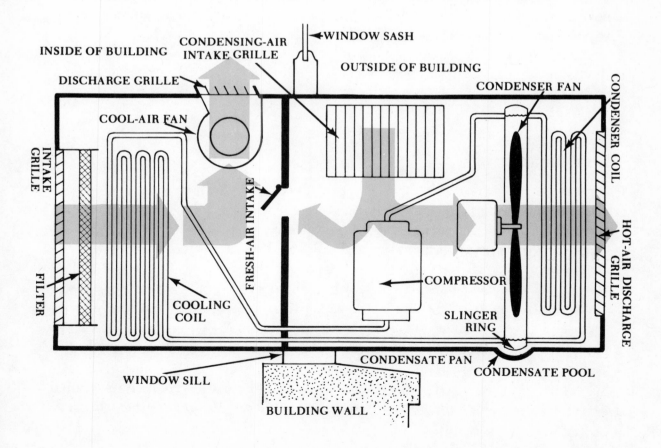

bottom of the ring rests in the pool of water. When the fan blade spins, water moves upward, completely covering the inside of the slinger ring. The moving fan knocks off drops of water that are blown against the hot coils of the condenser. This water evaporates, cooling the condenser coils and helping to change the refrigerant vapor within the condenser to a liquid. The water vapor is blown out of the air conditioner—to the outdoor air. The air blown out of the conditioner is replaced by outdoor air entering through a grill either in the top or the side of the outdoor compartment. Some of this entering air, however, goes through a small opening in the partition, and joins the air being blown into the room. This outdoor air is needed because the indoor fan sets up pressure within the room, and cool air seeps out of the room through the lower parts of doors and cracks where the wall meets the floor. If the air seeping out were not replaced by cool air from the conditioner, warm air would enter the room through the cracks above the doors and at the edges of the floor.

The term "central air conditioning" means that there is a large air conditioner somewhere in the building from which cool air is circulated throughout by fans pushing the air through wide metal channels called ducts. Narrower ducts branch off, taking conditioned air into each room. A second branching system of ducts transports air from the rooms back to the air conditioner.

An air conditioner is turned on and off by a thermostat. When the space to be cooled becomes warmer than the temperature set on the thermostat, the air conditioner goes on. When the air has been cooled to the temperature on the thermostat, the air conditioner goes off.

## HEATERS

### Convection

Heaters for homes and certain types of larger buildings usually employ a principle of physics known as *convection*—the transfer of heat by circulation currents in fluids such as gases and liquids. It works as follows: When fluids are heated, they expand, because the molecules of which they are composed move farther apart, taking up more space. This means that any unit of volume of fluid will contain fewer molecules when hot than when cold. Containing fewer molecules, a hot unit of volume will weigh less. For example, one liter of pure water at 4° C. will expand to 1.04 liters when heated to 95° C. The weight of a liter of pure water at 4° C. is 999.9 grams, and at 95° C. one liter weighs only 961.9 grams.

Suppose we place a lighted candle to one side underneath a goldfish bowl filled with water. The flame heats the water directly above it, and the heated water

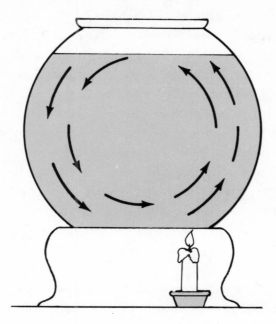

expands, becomes lighter, and rises *(follow the arrows in the illustration)*. It is important to understand that the lighter water does not simply rise by itself; the force of gravity pulls down more strongly on the surrounding cooler, heavier water which wedges under the warmer, lighter water, shoving it upward.

The rising water, moving away from the flame and coming in contact with cooler water, becomes cooler itself. It is pushed by a continuous stream of rising water over to the side of the bowl farthest from the candle. Being cooler and heavier, it sinks downward, and finally is pushed over to the point where the candle is heating water. Thus the first water to be heated has made a complete circuit of the fishbowl. The water continues in this circuit as long as the candle provides heat, and the heated water will eventually raise the temperature of all the water in the bowl. This transfer of heat by a circulating current is convection. Heated gases act the same as water, transferring heat by convection.

## Hot-Air Heater

A hot-air furnace, like all furnaces, has a chamber in which fuel is burned—the combustion chamber. In a furnace used for heating, it is usually made of iron. Surrounding the combustion chamber of a hot-air furnace is an air space enclosed by a metal jacket. The outside of the jacket is covered by some kind of heat-insulating material, usually asbestos. And this may be surrounded by sheet metal, which forms the outside of the furnace. In order for convection to work efficiently, the furnace is situated in the basement or on the bottom floor of a building.

There is an opening in the metal jacket that encloses the air space. This opening is at the top of the furnace, usually at the front, and joins a wide metal duct that runs up into the building between walls. The duct branches into every room. Another system of ducts branches from each room to a large return duct that descends between the walls to the bottom of the furnace at the rear.

The fuel may be coal, oil, or gas. The burning fuel produces hot gases and smoke which rise out of the furnace through a smoke outlet (a *flue*), and from this outlet up a chimney. Unfortunately, much of the heat produced by the fuel goes up the chimney with the hot gases, but before escaping, these gases transfer some of their heat to the sides and top of the combustion chamber. The heat easily passes by conduction through the iron to the air in the air-space. The heated air is pushed up the duct by convection, passes into the branching ducts, and then flows through openings in the floor or lower wall of each room. These openings usually have a metal grating with fins that can be opened and closed. When open, these gratings, called *registers*, let in the most air.

The warm air rises to the ceiling, cooling as it moves, and goes across the room. Now cool—and therefore heavy—the air sinks to the floor and passes down an outlet register. It then moves through a branch duct to the large descending duct that returns it to the bottom of the furnace at the rear, where it is reheated. Again and again it goes up into the house, continuing to circulate in this manner through convection.

## Forced Hot-Air Heater

A simple hot-air heating system such as the one just described does not warm evenly all the rooms in a house, and cannot be used in a large building. Although many older houses are still heated by a hot-air system, no such system is installed in houses or other buildings nowadays. Nevertheless, a hot-air system can be made quite efficient by redesigning the combustion chamber, adding electrical controls, and using the proper fuel. This type of heating system is called a *forced hot-air system*. This is how it works:

Thick iron plates, called *heat exchangers*, are placed in the combustion chamber and heated by the burning fuel, either oil or gas. A thermostat is placed in one of the rooms to be heated, and two more thermostats are placed in the furnace. A powerful fan is placed in the air space around the combustion chamber.

When the room in which the thermostat is located becomes cooler than the temperature set on the thermostat, an electrical signal goes from the thermostat to the furnace, lighting the burner. When the burning fuel has raised the heat exchangers to a certain temperature—in a house heater, usually between 125° and 140° F.—one of the thermostats (called the *fan control*) turns on the fan. This blows air over the heat exchangers, heating the air. The hot air is pushed through outlet ducts to registers in the floors or lower walls of rooms in the building. There

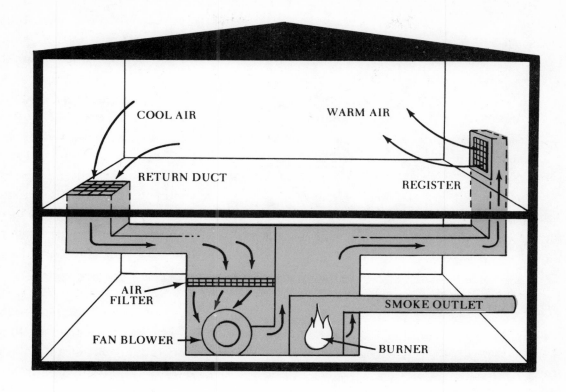

COOL AIR      WARM AIR

RETURN DUCT      REGISTER

AIR FILTER

SMOKE OUTLET

FAN BLOWER

BURNER

are no individual return registers. Instead, in a two-story house, for example, there is usually one large return register—containing a dust filter—at the top of the stairs, and a similar one at the bottom. From the return registers, air moves through return ducts to the furnace, where it is reheated so it can begin again its journey through the house.

Meanwhile, the burner is continuing to raise the temperature of the heat exchangers. When they reach a certain temperature (about 200° F.), a third thermostat, called an *upper limit control,* shuts off the burner. The fan continues to circulate heated air through the building. But this air takes heat from the heat exchangers, cooling them. When they have cooled to the temperature at which the fan started, the fan control thermostat shuts off the fan.

If the temperature of the room in which the thermostat is located has risen higher than the setting on the thermostat, the burner and fan remain off until the room cools. But if more heat is needed, the thermostat signals the furnace again, and the whole cycle—the actions of the fuel burner, heat exchangers, thermostats, and fan—starts all over again, until the room temperature is raised to the temperature set on the room thermostat.

Fuel is saved by the use of oil or gas burners which can be turned on and off by thermostats. And the push of the powerful fan distributes warm air around a room far more rapidly and thoroughly than air moved simply by convection. A forced-air heating system can be used to heat large buildings such as factories, garages, and airplane hangars, but is not usually used for tall buildings.

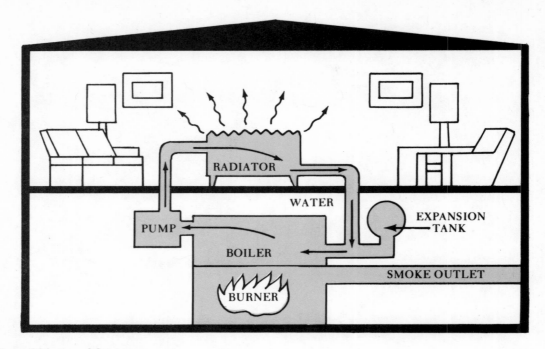

## Hot-Water Heater

The space surrounding the combustion chamber of a hot-water furnace is filled with water. A large outlet pipe rises from the furnace and smaller pipes branch out from it, running between the walls and floors into each room. The branch pipes are connected to radiators. One common kind of radiator is a heavy iron structure made up of a series of hollow chambers, called *coils,* which are linked together near the top and bottom. Near the bottom, an inlet pipe enters one end of the radiator, and an outlet pipe leaves the other end. The outlet pipe branches into a return pipe that runs down to the water-filled space around the combustion chamber.

Water heated by the burning fuel rises in the furnace outlet pipe and enters the radiators. Because the water is hot and therefore light, it rises to the top of each radiator coil, giving off heat which first passes through the iron. Air adjoining the hot radiator is warmed and rises toward the ceiling, beginning a journey around the room. Because a radiator initiates the convection of air in a room, a radiator is sometimes called a convector. In addition to heating the air, a radiator also warms people and objects in a room by radiating heat waves to them.

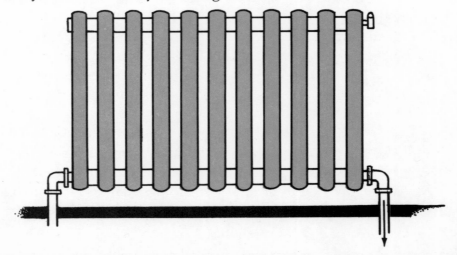

Having given off its heat, the water in the upper part of the radiator becomes cool and sinks to the bottom. From there it runs out of the radiator through the outlet pipe. The cooled water eventually returns to the furnace where it begins its round-trip journey again.

Water cannot be compressed easily. Since the water in a hot-water system expands when heated, some method must be used to prevent the expanding water from bursting the furnace jacket, pipes or radiators. This is accomplished by connecting to the furnace a small tank, called an *expansion tank*. This tank is about half-filled with water. The other half contains air which, unlike water, is elastic and is easily compressed. When the water in the heating system expands, it pushes into the expansion tank, compressing the air and relieving pressure on the rest of the system.

Hot-water systems that rely on convection to circulate heated water through pipes and radiators usually do not do a good job of warming buildings that are more than two stories high. However, there is a way to make a hot-water heating system work well in buildings a few stories taller: by using a pump to circulate the water rapidly, and thermostats to turn a gas or oil burner on and off. Instead of coil radiators, a single iron pipe runs along the baseboard on one side of a room. The pipe is surrounded along its length by a series of metal fins which increases the area of hot metal radiating heat to the room. Today, even two-story houses often use the pump-circulated, gas-fired or oil-fired hot-water heating systems.

The main advantage of hot-water heating is the steadiness of the heat. Once a room has been warmed to the desired temperature, the hot water maintains the heat for a long time. This also results in a saving of fuel.

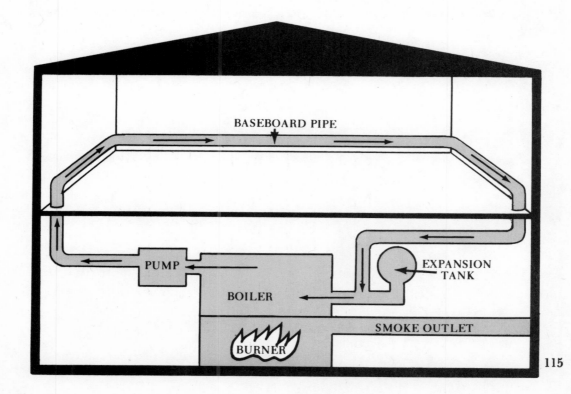

## Radiant Heating System

A radiant heating system is a kind of hot-water system that does not use radiators that take up space in each room. Instead, pipes arranged in a continuous zigzag formation are embedded in the floors of the rooms. When installing a radiant heating system, a builder first constructs the zigzag, placing it in the proper position. Concrete is then poured over the pipes, burying them an inch or two beneath the surface. One end of the pipe structure leaves one end of the furnace; the other end returns to the opposite side. Water then circulates from the furnace, beneath the floor, and back to the furnace. Since radiant heat is usually not used in buildings more than one story tall, convection cannot be relied upon as a force to circulate the water. A pump at the furnace is therefore connected to the pipe zigzag to drive hot water through the pipes.

As the hot water circulates, it gives off heat to the pipes and the pipes heat the floor. The warm floor radiates heat to the air, and to the people and objects in the room.

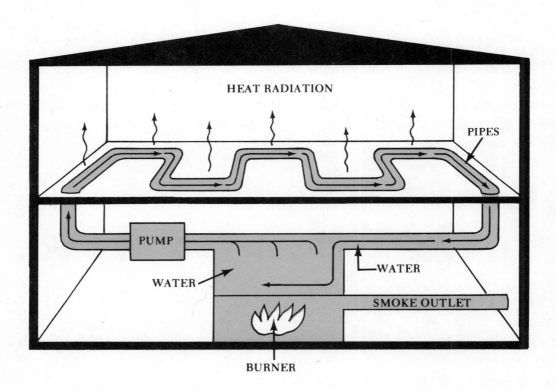

## Steam Heating System

A steam heating system is much like a hot-water system. The main differences are that only the space surrounding the combustion chamber is filled with water, and that this water is boiled. (This is why the furnace is usually called a boiler.) When the water boils, it fills the pipes and radiators with steam.

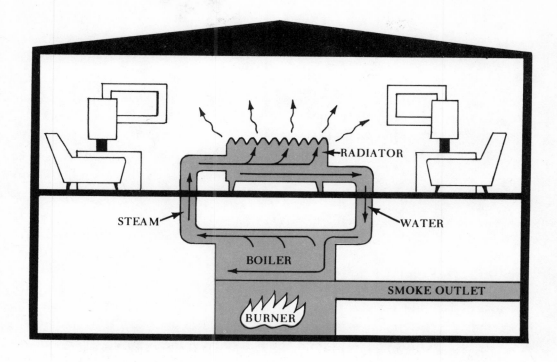

Upon transferring its heat to a radiator, steam cools and condenses to water. The water collects at the bottom of the radiator and then runs through the pipes down to the boiler. Some steam-heat systems have only one pipe connected to each radiator, in which case the pipe must be wide enough to allow the steam to rise at the same time water is draining from the radiators and running down to the boiler. Other steam systems have two sets of pipes, one for the rising steam and the other for the returning water.

One of the problems of a steam-heat system is air in the radiators. Dissolved air boils out of water in the boiler, and some air seeps in through very small cracks in the joints which connect the pipes. The air within the system collects in the upper parts of radiators. If air were allowed to remain, radiators would eventually become completely filled with air, which would keep out steam. However, air is removed by means of a valve attached to each radiator near the top of the coil farthest from the inlet pipe. The valve allows air to escape and prevents its return. But the valve shuts when steam enters it, preventing escape of the steam.

Another problem of steam-heating is its unevenness. The radiators are usually either sizzling hot or as cool as the room in which they are located. On cold days, when fuel is burned rapidly, the water boils vigorously. Steam is sent rushing through the pipes and radiators, which become very hot. On mild days, when it is desirable to have the radiators not much warmer than room temperature, it is difficult to keep the whole system of pipes and radiators filled with steam, and yet not become too hot. One solution to this problem is to have a hand-operated gate

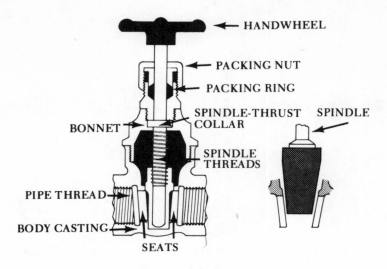

## GATE VALVE

Labels: HANDWHEEL, PACKING NUT, PACKING RING, SPINDLE-THRUST COLLAR, SPINDLE, BONNET, SPINDLE THREADS, PIPE THREAD, BODY CASTING, SEATS

valve on the inlet pipe of each radiator. Someone then opens or closes each valve, letting just enough steam flow into the radiator to keep it at the desired temperature. Regulating the heat of a radiator in this manner is difficult and bothersome. If the furnace is regulated by a thermostat, the radiators are alternately heated quite hot and then allowed to cool, maintaining the rooms at an average temperature which is close to the desired temperature.

The main advantage of steam heat is that it can be used to heat even tall buildings. Air is eliminated from the heating system through air valves. The pressure within the system is kept low by means of a suction pump. This low pressure allows steam to push easily into every part of the system, including the upper stories of tall buildings.

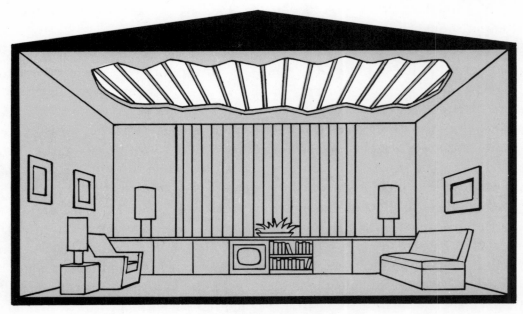

ELECTRIC HEATING

## Electric Heating System

An electric heating system consists of a network of insulated wires placed in the ceiling of each room. *(See illustration at bottom of previous page.)* Electric current flowing through the wires causes them to become hot. Heat waves radiate downward, warming the air, people, and objects in the room. Each room has a separate network from the others and is controlled by its own thermostat; thus, each room can be kept at a different temperature, if desired. Electric heating can be used in buildings of any height or size.

## Thermostat

A thermostat is an automatic device which regulates temperature by turning a source of heat on and off, such as a gas burner in a furnace.

The most widely used kind of thermostat has as its main working part a bimetallic bar. This bar is made up of two thin strips of different kinds of metal; for example, iron and copper. The strips are joined along their entire length. Both strips expand (when heated) and contract (when cooled) at different rates. Since

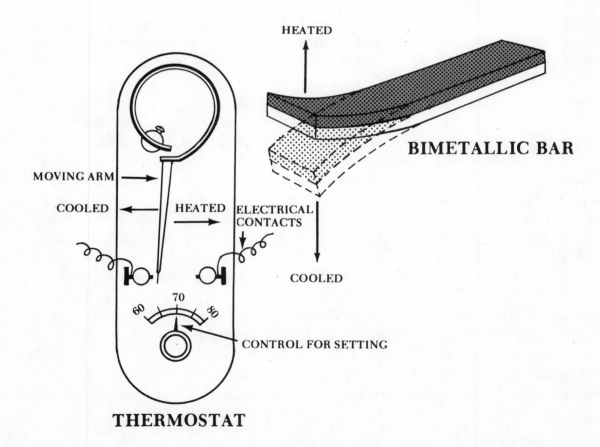

MOVING ARM

COOLED ← → HEATED ELECTRICAL CONTACTS

CONTROL FOR SETTING

**THERMOSTAT**

HEATED

COOLED

**BIMETALLIC BAR**

the two strips are tightly joined, the different rates of expansion cause the bimetallic bar to warp, or bend. Thus, the bar may be either straight or bent into a curve that will best fit its use.

In a thermostat, one end of the bimetallic bar is held immovable and is connected to one part of an electric circuit. The circuit runs from the thermostat to the heat source and back to the thermostat. The other end of the strip is free to bend as the temperature changes. Near the free end is a contact, also part of the electric circuit. When a change in temperature causes the bimetallic bar to bend far enough to touch the contact, the electrical circuit is completed, and the heat source is turned on. After the heat source has produced enough heat to change the temperature of the bimetallic bar, the bar straightens, breaking the electrical contact. This opens the circuit, thereby shutting off the heat source.

The fixed end of the bar can be connected to a dial. Turning the dial moves the bar so that the gap between its free end and the contact is widened or narrowed. A wide gap requires the bar to bend farther before touching the contact. To cause the bar to move farther requires a greater change in temperature. This means, for example, that a room must be heated to a higher temperature to cause the bar to close the gap.

The designers of a thermostat experiment to find out how much the bar moves for a one-degree change in temperature. Knowing this, they can mark the dial with numbers representing degrees of temperature. Then the dial can be turned so that the marking on the dial, representing the temperature you want, is even with a fixed line on the casing of the thermostat. This is called "setting the thermostat." By setting the thermostat at the temperature you want, the thermostat will turn on the heat source when the room becomes cooler than the desired temperature. Then, when the room has reached that temperature, the thermostat shuts off the heat.

An improvement on the room thermostat just described is the use of a metal spiral, which may or may not be bimetallic. Attached to the uppermost part of the spiral is a small glass vial half-filled with mercury *(see illustration on next page)*, a metal that is a liquid. The circuit has two wires running into one end of the vial and separated by a small gap. Changes in temperature cause the spiral to expand or contract, tipping the vial first in one direction, then in the opposite direction. When the vial is tipped one way, all the mercury runs into its lowest part. If this is the end containing the wires, the mercury bridges the gap between the wires. Since mercury can conduct electricity, the electrical circuit is completed, and the heat source is turned on. When the room is hot enough, the metal spiral expands and tips the vial in the opposite direction. The mercury runs to the other end of the vial, leaving a gap between the wires, thus breaking the circuit and shutting off the heat source.

The advantage of the mercury-vial thermostat is that it gives a quick, accurate contact. The bimetallic bar, in comparison, expands so slowly that before it

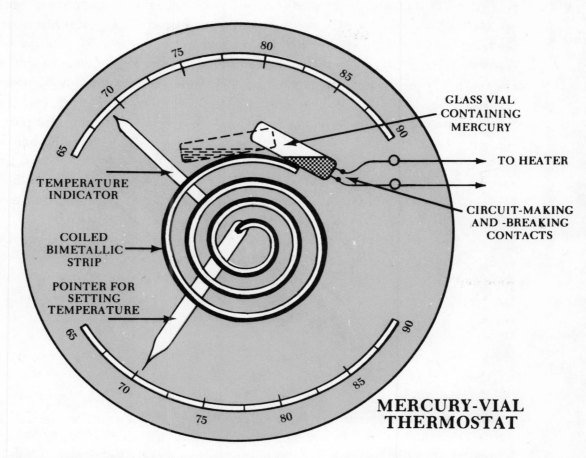

**MERCURY-VIAL THERMOSTAT**

Labels on diagram:
- 75 80 85 90 65 70 65 70 75 80 85 90
- GLASS VIAL CONTAINING MERCURY
- TO HEATER
- CIRCUIT-MAKING AND -BREAKING CONTACTS
- TEMPERATURE INDICATOR
- COILED BIMETALLIC STRIP
- POINTER FOR SETTING TEMPERATURE

touches the contact, electric current jumps the gap, and this jumping spark, called an arc, eats away the contact. Also, since the spark jumps before the contact should be made, this type of thermostat is not very accurate.

# EVERYDAY THINGS

## BALLPOINT PEN

The ballpoint pen has been in use for about twenty-five years. This seems a long time, but in the history of writing a ballpoint pen is really very new. Thousands of years ago writing was done with berry-juice as ink and a split sliver of bamboo, or coarse animal-hairs attached to a stick, or perhaps just a pointed twig, for the writing instrument.

A ballpoint pen is simply a long, narrow plastic or metal tube containing sticky ink, a smaller, thinner tube, and a small metal ball. The tube—only one-tenth of an inch in diameter—is too thin to be held comfortably for writing, so it is surrounded by a thicker plastic or metal tube, called the *body*. The ink tube is also called the *ink reservoir*.

The ink in the tube is about as firm and sticky as jelly. It is kept from oozing out of the bottom of the tube by a smaller, narrower metal tube about one six-hundredth of an inch wide, which is attached to the bottom. The front end of the thinner tube is blocked by a steel ball four one-hundredths of an inch in diameter. The ball is held in place by a narrowing of the tube just in front of and in back of it.

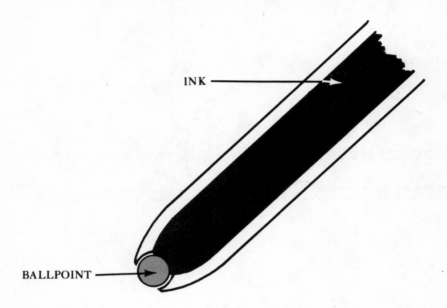

INK

BALLPOINT

The ball is free to move in any direction, and it does this as the pen itself is moved across a piece of paper. As the ball revolves, it rubs on the ink behind it, and some ink sticks to the ball. As the ball rolls over the paper, it transfers ink to the paper. Since the pen is usually pointing downward, gravity pulls the ink down, and ink is always in contact with the ball. If you try to write with the pen pointing upward, you will find that no ink comes out after you have written a few words. This happens because gravity is pulling the ink away from the ball. If you leave a ballpoint pen on its side or with its point upward for several hours or days, you will have to roll its point on paper for a foot or two before gravity pulls the ink down to the ball and some ink sticks to the ball. Even if the ball point has been pointing down, the pen may not begin to write as soon as you roll the ball on paper. If you look closely, you will see a very short inkless dent where the ball pushed into the paper, but no ink was transferred to the paper. This happens because ink dried on the half of the ball exposed to the air, and the ball had to turn at least half a turn before it could bring ink to the paper.

Ballpoint pens that write immediately upon being rolled on paper have a ball made from a number of particles of a hard material that are compressed and baked, so that they stick together. This kind of ball has many very small channels into which ink oozes on all sides. Even when the pen is not being used, there is ink on the outer half of the ball; this enables the pen to write at any time.

The ink tube of some ballpoint pens is covered simply by a wider tube of plastic. Most of the pens that are made to be carried in a pocket or purse are *retractable* ballpoint pens; that is, the ink tube is contained in a plastic or metal body that has in it a device for pulling the ball point into the body when the pen is not in use. When you push a button on the top of the pen, the ball point is pushed out of the body and stays out when you release the button. When you push the button a second time, the point springs back into the body. There is more than one way to accomplish this, but in all retractable ballpoint pens, the first push on the button not only pushes the point out of the body, but engages a catch that holds the point out. The second push releases the catch, and a spring at the front of the body moves the ink tube with its ball back into the body.

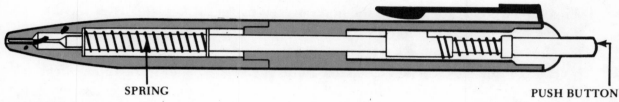

SPRING                                                              PUSH BUTTON

## LOCKS

### Rim Lock

The simplest kind of lock is a *rim lock*. Its working parts are attached to a metal plate called a *backplate* that is fastened by screws into a rectangular hole cut into the edge of a door. Opposite this part of the lock is a small rectangular hole cut in the wood of the doorframe. A hole is drilled in the side of the door; this hole opens to the working parts of the lock. The hole is covered by a metal plate with an irregular-shaped hole—the *keyhole*. Attached to the side of the key at one end is a piece of metal, the *bit*, shaped to fit into the keyhole. Sliding along the surface of the plate is a flat, specially shaped piece of metal, called a *tumbler*. Moving to

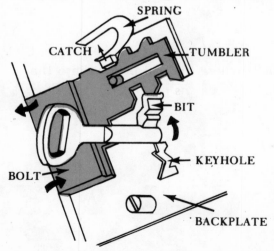

SOME SHAPES OF KEY BITS

either one of two positions, the tumbler is held in place by a catch attached to a spring. In front of the tumbler is a tough, hard piece of metal, the *bolt*.

To close the lock, you must have a key that will fit the keyhole. Once the key is in the hole, its shape and size must enable it to push the tumbler when the key is turned. The proper key pushes the tumbler past the catch and against the bolt. The bolt is pushed past the edge of the backplate and into the hole in the doorframe. The outside of this hole is covered by a metal plate, the *strikeplate*, which has a rectangular hole into which the bolt fits exactly. Once the bolt is in the hole, the door cannot be opened, because the bolt is a single strong piece of metal bridging the space between the edge of the door and the doorframe. The catch on the backplate prevents the bolt from slipping back if the door is shaken. The strikeplate prevents the door from being opened by a moderate force that would break the wood at the edge of the hole covered by the strikeplate. After the door is locked, the key can be pulled slightly away from the tumbler and turned so that it can be removed from the keyhole.

To open the lock, the key is inserted into the keyhole and turned in a direction opposite to that which closed the lock. This pushes the tumbler and attached bolt into the door, and the door can be opened.

## Rim Lock With Several Tumblers

It is not difficult to open a single-tumbler rim lock. To make a lock harder for an intruder to open, three or four tumblers may be used. The tumblers are thin and lie on top of each other. The backplate has a metal projection called a *pin*. The tumblers have an irregularly shaped notch cut in them, and the projections in the notch prevent the tumblers from moving past the pin. The key bit also has projections. When the key is inserted into the lock and turned, the projections on the bit move each tumbler just far enough so that it can slip past the pin. The action of the bolt itself is the same as in a single-tumbler rim lock.

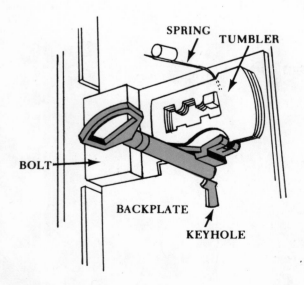

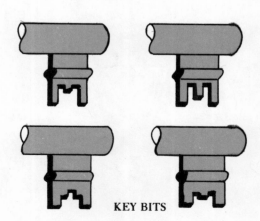

KEY BITS

## Ward and Tumbler Lock

To make the opening of a lock even more difficult for an intruder, the backplate may have curved pieces of metal, called *wards*, past which the key must move. To do this, the key must have notches that will fit around the wards. The combined use of several tumblers and several wards makes the lock quite difficult to open by a person who does not have the right key.

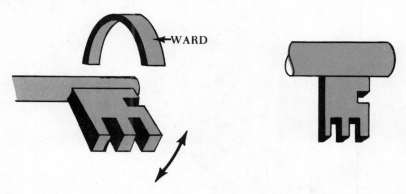

## Cylinder Lock

Probably the most widely used lock is the *cylinder lock*. A metal barrel surrounds a metal *cylinder*, or *plug*. (*See illustration below.*) In the upper part of the barrel are several small cylindrical pieces of metal called *pins*. Each pin is made in two pieces. The spring is in contact with the top of the upper piece. The bottom of the upper piece is round and rests on the flat top of the lower piece. The bottom of the lower piece tapers to a blunt point. The pins are pushed by springs down into holes in the cylinder. The key is flat and has slots in its sides. The slots enable the key to fit into projections in an irregularly shaped keyhole. The upper edge of the key is irregularly notched.

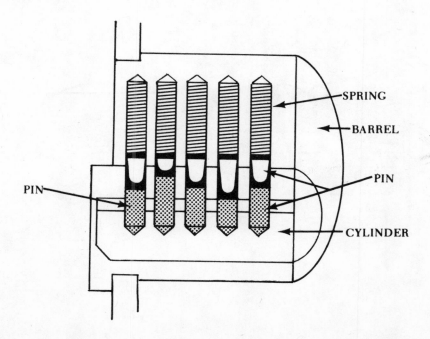

When the pins are pushed down into the cylinder, they prevent the cylinder from turning. *(See previous illustration.)* When a key with the proper set of notches is inserted into the cylinder, however, the pointed bottoms of the pins fit into the notches, which are the proper height to make the tops of the lower parts of the pins form a straight line right at the surface of the cylinder. It is then possible to turn the cylinder.

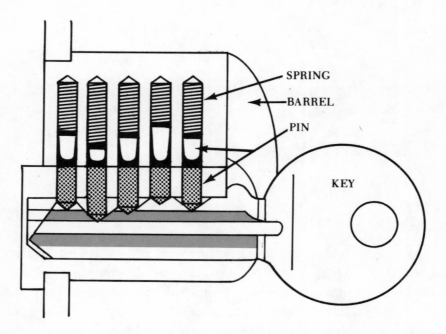

If a key with the proper side slots, but wrong notches, is inserted into the cylinder, the pins do not line up evenly with the surface of the cylinder and the cylinder cannot be turned.

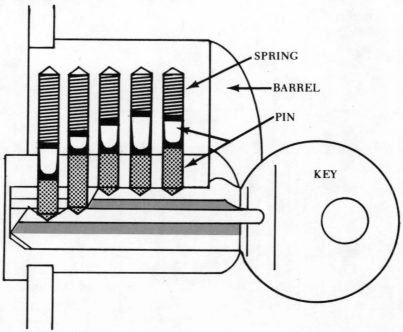

The cylinder is attached to a bolt, which moves into the door when the key is turned. Many cylinder locks have a spring attached to the bolt, which is beveled on the side toward the outside of the door. This is a *spring latch*. To lock it, you need only close the door. The spring forces the beveled bolt into the hole behind the strikeplate. If the bolt is not on a spring, it is not beveled, and to lock this kind of lock, called a *dead lock* or *dead latch*, you must turn the key in the direction opposite to that which locked it.

## Combination Lock

You may use a *combination padlock* on your school locker or your bicycle. This kind of lock opens without a key. You turn a dial to line up in proper order three numbers on a dial with a mark on the face of the lock. Or, you may turn a pointer that moves past numbers on a stationary dial. The proper numbers and their order are the combination of the lock.

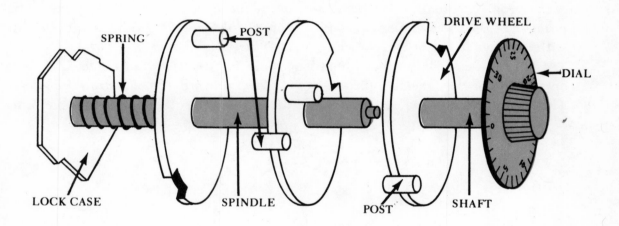

Inside the lock are three small wheels. One of the wheels, the *drive wheel*, is attached to a *shaft*, so that it turns with the dial. The other two wheels turn freely around a *spindle*. One end of the spindle fits into the drive wheel; the other end is attached to a flat piece of metal called the *lock case*. A spring keeps the shaft pushed into the spindle. (Some locks have the shaft and spindle arranged differently.)

Each wheel has a slot in its edge. Wheel No. 1 and the drive wheel both have a post sticking out from the face toward the center wheel. The center wheel has a post on both faces. Wheel No. 1 and wheel No. 2 will turn only when their post is pushed by the wheel next to it.

127

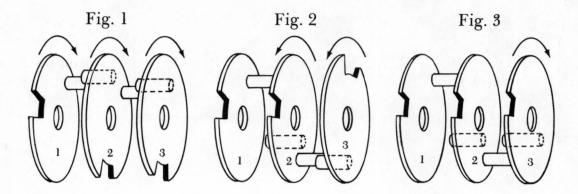

Fig. 1      Fig. 2      Fig. 3

To open the lock, you first turn the dial all the way around twice, either to the left or the right. This moves the posts of all three wheels together, so that they all turn with the dial. Next, you turn the dial to the first number of the combination. This sets the slot in wheel No. 1 in a certain position. *(See illustration above, Fig. 1.)*

Then you turn the dial one full turn in the opposite direction and continue on to the second number. As you do this, wheel No. 1 does not turn, but wheel No. 2 turns so that its slot is lined up with the slot on wheel No. 1. *(See illustration above, Fig. 2.)* Finally, you turn the dial in the opposite direction to the third number of the combination. This turns only the drive wheel, and lines its slot up with the slots in the other two wheels. *(See illustration above, Fig. 3.)*

A tug on the *shackle*—the curved bar—pulls it partway out of the lock. A hook on one end of the shackle pulls the *locking lever* upward. *(See illustration below.)* This lever turns on a pin through its middle, pushing the other end of the lever into

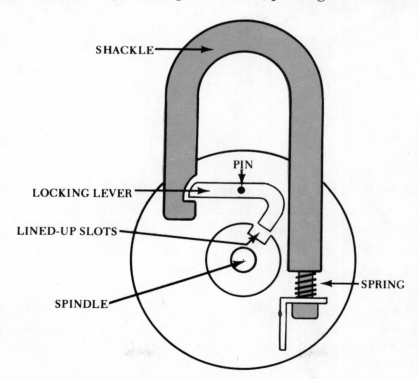

SHACKLE

PIN

LOCKING LEVER

LINED-UP SLOTS

SPINDLE

SPRING

the slots in the wheels. With the locking lever out of the way, the shackle can be pulled out of the lock.

When you push the shackle back into the lock, the hook pushes down on one end of the locking lever. This turns the other end out of the slots in the wheels. Then you spin the dial, breaking up the alignment of the slots. The lock cannot be opened until the slots are brought back into line.

A dial with thirty numbers can have 27,000 combinations of three numbers. It would take a very long time for a thief to discover the right combinations simply by trial and error.

## TOILET

As a toilet, or water closet, gets rid of waste materials, it acts as a siphon. A siphon is a tube in the form of an upside-down letter U, with one side longer than the other. Because of the pressure of the atmosphere on the surface of a liquid, a siphon can be used to drain the liquid up and over the wall of a container. *(See illustration below.)*

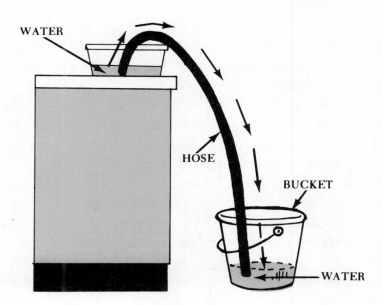

The bowl of a toilet is shaped like a wide funnel with a spout that is bent upward behind the bowl. The bowl, the spout, and the drainpipe into which the spout opens, all form a siphon.

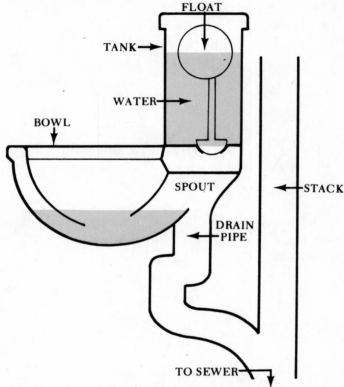

Most of the time, the bowl and the spout are partly filled with water. The water in the spout effectively seals off the bowl from the drainpipe and keeps unpleasant odors from entering the bathroom.

All around the bowl, beneath the wide rim, are holes. The rim itself forms the walls of a square tube into which the holes open. Behind and above the bowl is a tank that holds from four to six gallons of water. An opening in the bottom of the tank connects with the rim around the bowl.

When you flush the toilet, the water stored in the tank runs into the rim and through the holes into the bowl. The water rises until it runs over the rim of the spout and into the drainpipe. This begins a siphoning action that empties water and waste materials from the bowl into the drainpipe. *(See illustration at top of next page.)* The siphoning action continues until the bowl is empty; then some of the clear water that is left in the spout runs back into the bowl.

The drainpipe projects through the roof of the building and is open at the top. Air pressing down from the stack counters the air pressure on the water in the bowl. This stops the siphon action when the bowl is empty and also leaves some water in the spout.

It is easy to see first-hand how the tank works. Lift the top off the tank and flush the water. The flush lever outside the tank is connected to one inside. The other end of the inside flush lever is attached to a thin metal rod that connects

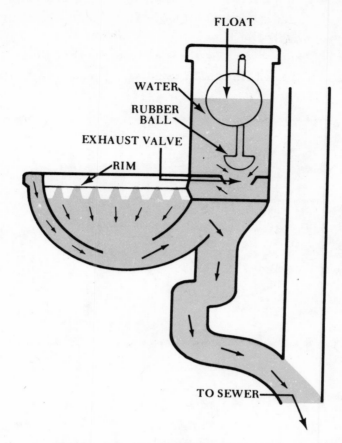

FLOAT

WATER

RUBBER
BALL

EXHAUST VALVE

RIM

TO SEWER

downward by means of wire or flat-metal guides to a half-round or a pear-shaped rubber ball with a hole in the bottom. The ball and the hole it fits into make up the *exhaust valve*. Moving the flush lever sideways lifts the part of the flush lever that is inside the tank. This, in turn, lifts the rod, which pulls up the rubber ball from a wide hole in which it rests. The water runs out of the tank and into the bowl through the holes around the rim.

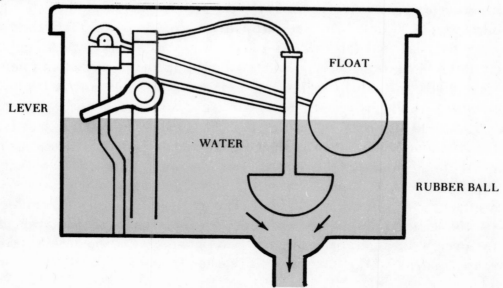

FLOAT

LEVER

WATER

RUBBER BALL

When the tank is filled, a hollow ball made of thin metal floats on the surface of the water. The ball, called a *float*, is attached by a metal rod to an intake valve. As soon as water flows out of the tank, the floating ball moves downward with the lowering surface. It thereby causes the rod to open the intake valve, and water begins to run into the tank through a metal tube that opens at the bottom of the tank.

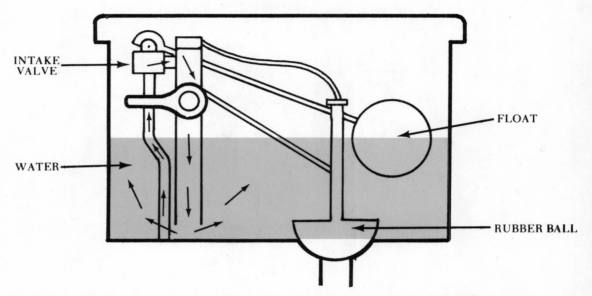

When the tank is nearly empty, the rubber ball drops into the hole, closing the exhaust valve. Water entering the intake valve continues to run into the tank. As the water rises, the float rises with it, and when the water level reaches about three-quarters of the height of the tank, the float has risen high enough so that the rod attached to it closes the intake valve. The toilet is ready to be flushed again.

## SELF-SERVICE PASSENGER ELEVATOR

A passenger elevator is a box, called a *car*, that carries people from one floor to another inside a building. The car moves up and down within a *shaft*, a rectangular space extending from the bottom to the top of the building. The car itself fits within a strong metal *frame* that moves up and down between *guide rails* attached to the sides of the shaft. An electric motor provides most of the power for lifting the car; and gravity pulls it down. The motor turns a grooved wheel, or *drive sheave*, located above the top of the shaft. Steel cables run up the shaft from the top of the frame holding the car, then over the drive sheave and down the back of the shaft to a *counterweight*. This is a stack of wide, thick iron bars that weigh almost as much as the car and frame. The counterweight moves between guide rails attached to the back of the shaft. The downward pull of the counterweight helps the motor pull the car up. The downward pull of both the car and counterweight press the cables tightly into the grooves of the drive sheave. This pressure insures that the cables will move when the sheave turns.

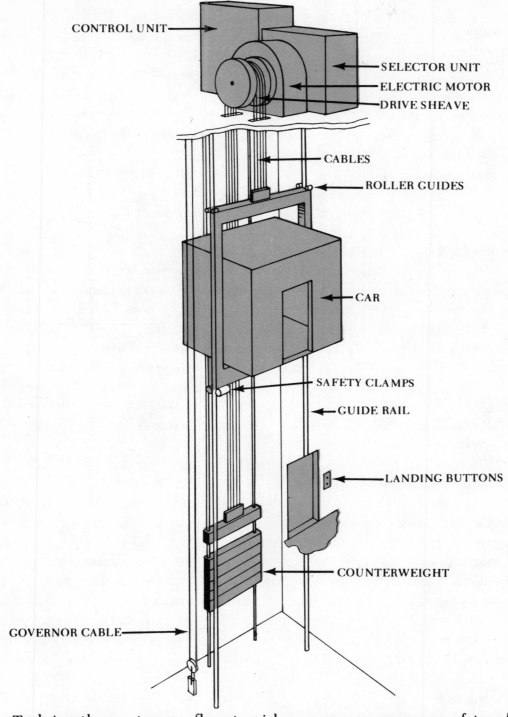

CONTROL UNIT

SELECTOR UNIT

ELECTRIC MOTOR

DRIVE SHEAVE

CABLES

ROLLER GUIDES

CAR

SAFETY CLAMPS

GUIDE RAIL

LANDING BUTTONS

COUNTERWEIGHT

GOVERNOR CABLE

To bring the car to your floor to pick you up, you press one of two *landing buttons* located on each floor near the door of the elevator. You press the upper button if you want to go up, the lower button if you want to go down. Inside the car is one or more rows of buttons, each button corresponding to a floor of the building. Pushing a button sends electric current to a *selector unit* and a *control unit*, both located above the top of the shaft. The selector unit acts as a computer, sorts out the calls made by button-pushers, and then "tells" the control unit how and when to move the drive sheave and to open and close the elevator doors. The selector makes sure that a car going down does not stop to pick up a passenger who wants to go up. Also, the selector stops the cars in the proper order of the floors to which the passengers want to go. For example, a car may be at the third floor on the way up. Someone on the ninth floor pushes an "up" button a moment before another person on the fifth floor pushes an "up" button. The selector ensures that the car will not go straight to the ninth floor, passing the person on the fifth floor who pushed the button a moment later.

As a car approaches a floor at which it is to stop, the control slows the car to a smooth halt. When the car has stopped, a door on the car opens, as does a door in the shaft. To a passenger waiting for the elevator, the shaft door is a door in the wall. If the inner door does not open, the outer door will remain closed. Neither door will open if the floor of the car and the floor of the story at which the car has stopped are not on the same level. The doors are held open for a few seconds—to allow passengers to enter or leave—by a timing device working either through the control unit or through a photoelectric cell called a *photocell*. The photocell is located in the wall between the inner and outer doors, and its light beam crosses the opened door. The beam is broken by passengers entering and leaving the car. The timing device is set to close the door a predetermined number of seconds after the beam is intact again. Each time the beam is broken, the closing is delayed the same number of seconds. This makes it possible for passengers to enter or leave the car without having the door close before they are all inside or out. Both doors must close securely, or the elevator will not start.

In addition to the safety provided by the proper opening and closing of doors, there are other safety devices on elevators. A steel cable attached to the side of the car turns the speed governor, which is above the top of the shaft. If the car moves too rapidly, the governor spins so fast that metal balls attached to a central rod move outward far enough to throw a switch. The switch lets electric current into a device that presses a brake on the drive sheave. If the brake cannot slow the car enough, the governor grips the *governor cable*. This releases safety clamps on the car which wedge against the guide rails, bringing the car to a stop.

## AUTOMATIC WASHING MACHINE

An automatic washing machine is one that washes and rinses clothes and takes most of the water out of them, leaving them ready for drying. The machine performs these tasks in a certain order and for a measured time without anyone having to adjust it. The washing cycle begins after you have "told" the washing machine what to do by setting two dials and closing a switch.

There are two different types of automatic washers: the *front-loading*, or *cylinder*, into which clothes are put through a door at the front of the machine; and the *top-loading*, or *agitator*, into which clothes are put through a door at the top.

**FRONT-LOADING
CYLINDER TYPE**

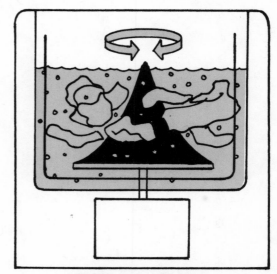

**TOP-LOADING
AGITATOR TYPE**

Clothes put into a front-loading washer lie in a porcelain-enameled steel cylinder pierced by rows of holes. The cylinder, which is on its side, revolves in a large tub almost half-full of water. Within the cylinder there are usually four shelflike ridges, called *baffles*, that run the length of the cylinder. During washing and rinsing, the cylinder revolves continually. The baffles push the clothes through the water, carrying them out of the water and upward until gravity causes the clothes to fall back; the process is then repeated. The tumbling action continues until the clothes are thoroughly washed.

Clothes in a top-loading washer lie in an upright, porcelain-enameled cylinder with a bottom. The cylinder is pierced by rows of holes and stands in a large tub. In the center of the cylinder, but not attached to it, is an *agitator*, a hard-rubber or tough plastic cone with blades, or fins, protruding outward. The agitator fits over a central shaft. During washing and rinsing, the shaft and agitator turn back and forth continually. The blades catch the clothes and swish them around. This movement also creates currents in the water, which improve the washing. There are many different kinds of agitators, but the way they work is basically the same.

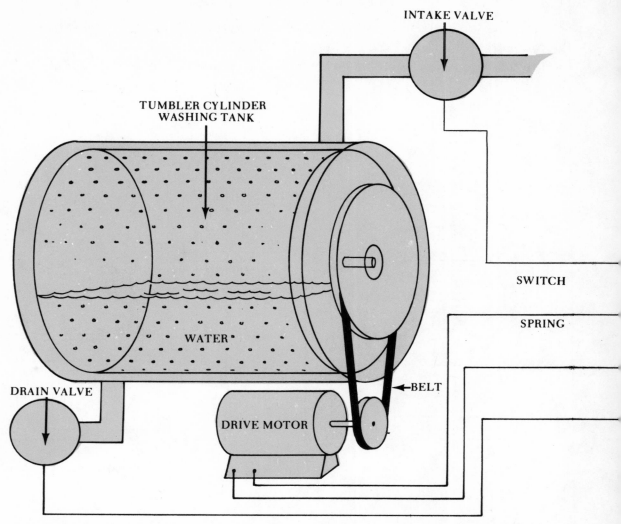

INTAKE VALVE

TUMBLER CYLINDER
WASHING TANK

WATER

SWITCH

SPRING

DRAIN VALVE

BELT

DRIVE MOTOR

After clothes and a measured amount of soap powder are put into a washer, the temperature of the washing water and rinsing water are chosen by either setting a dial, pushing buttons, or moving switch levers, depending on the particular washer. In the same manner, the amount of water in the tub can be set; there is no reason to use as much water for a small or medium-sized wash as for a large one. Then the control dial is set; this dial lets the operator choose how long the clothes will be washed, rinsed, and spun. Finally, the motor that turns the cylinder or agitator is switched on, usually by pushing or pulling a knob in the center of the control dial, or, in a coin-operated laundry, by putting a coin into the coin slot.

During the time that clothes are in the washer, which can be anywhere from ten minutes to half an hour, four different things happen: (1) water runs into the tub and fills the cylinder; (2) the cylinder revolves or the agitator moves back and forth; (3) water drains out of the washer; (4) the cylinder spins rapidly.

Some of these operations take longer than others. Sometimes two are going on at the same time. Each operation is started and stopped by a switch in an automatic-control unit which programs the operations according to the way the water temperature, water level, and timing dials are set.

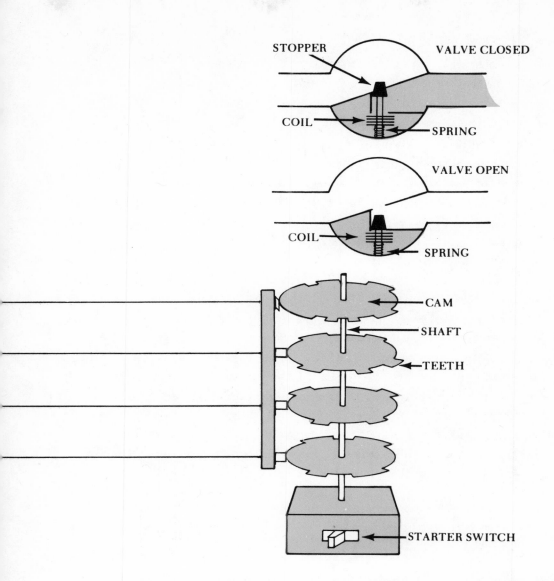

STOPPER · VALVE CLOSED

COIL · SPRING

VALVE OPEN

COIL · SPRING

CAM

SHAFT

TEETH

STARTER SWITCH

Timing is accomplished by a *timer unit* which is set in motion when the motor is switched on or coins are put into the slot. The timer has a small *timing motor*. The speed of this motor, greatly lessened by gears, turns a long shaft very slowly. Attached to the shaft are four *cams*. In a washer, the cams are discs with squared-off projections, or teeth. At the level of each cam is a switch that controls one of the washer's four operations.

As the cams begin to turn, a tooth on one cam pushes down a switch that sends electric current to the *intake valve*. This valve consists of a stopper, or plunger, that fits tightly into a hole in a barrier across the water-intake pipe. The stopper is attached to the short iron rod that fits within a coil of wire. When current enters the coil, it acts as an electromagnet, pulling the stopper out of the hole, and lets water into the washer. Meanwhile, none of the teeth on any of the other cams are in contact with switches. The cam holding down the switch turns slowly. When the end of the first tooth is reached, a spring pushes up the switch, which cuts off electric current from the electromagnet, and a powerful spring snaps the plug back into the water-intake hole, shutting off the flow of water into the tub.

Next, the first tooth on the second cam pushes down a switch that turns on the *drive motor*. Depending on the type of washer, the motor either revolves the cylinder or, by an arrangement of gears, causes the agitator to turn back and forth. When the cam turns to the end of the tooth, the switch springs back, and no more current flows into the motor, which stops the washing action.

After a few seconds, a third cam pushes down a switch that starts the motor again. At the same time, a fourth cam pushes a switch that opens the *drain valve*, which operates like the water-intake valve. In the cylinder type of washer, the motor begins to turn the cylinder slowly, but picks up speed until it is spinning rapidly. In the agitator type of washer, the cylinder (but not the agitator) begins to spin, gaining speed as it turns. In both types of washers, spinning causes centrifugal force, which forces water against the sides of the cylinder. Since the sides are pierced by holes, water flows through them into the tub. The drain valve is open, so water runs out of the tub, into a drainpipe, and onward to the sewer. When all the wash water is out of the tub, the cylinder is spinning very fast. Water in the fibers of the clothes is thrown toward the sides of the cylinder and then into the tub. By the time the third cam switches off the motor, the clothes are about two-thirds dry. At the same time the motor is switched off, the fourth cam allows the drain valve to snap shut.

The first cam now lets fresh water into the washer to rinse soap out of the clothes. And all the other cams repeat the actions they took when the clothes were being washed. After the final spin, you take the nearly dry clothes out of the washer and finish drying them in an automatic dryer or on a clothesline.

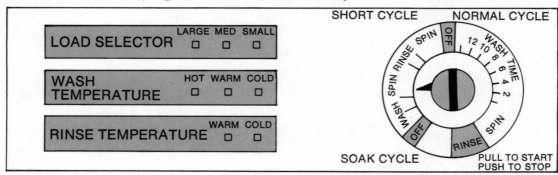

An automatic dishwasher works in much the same way as an agitator-type automatic clothes washer. Cams let water into and out of the washing chamber that contains the dirty dishes and silverware. An agitator swishes hot soapy water over the things being washed.

There are, of course, differences between a clothes washer and a dishwasher. In a dishwasher, a small pump sends water into the washing chamber and drains it out. There is no cylinder in a dishwasher; the dishes and silverware are not spun dry. They are dried by an electric heating coil that is enclosed in a metal tube in the shape of a loop. The hot loop, located at the bottom of the washing chamber, heats the air inside the dishwasher, and the hot air evaporates water from the things that were washed and rinsed.

138

# GLOSSARY

This glossary contains technical terms used in the text but not defined. It also contains words defined in one part of the text and used in another part without definition.

**a.c.:** *See* alternating current.

**alloy:** A solution or mixture of two or more metals.

**alternating current:** Electric current that rapidly, continually, and periodically reverses its direction of flow. Abbreviated a.c. or A.C.

**AM:** A system of radio broadcasting in which the amplitude of the waves of a carrier frequency is varied, or modulated, above and below its normal level. AM stands for *amplitude modulation*. *See also* FM, audio frequency, carrier frequency.

**ampere:** A unit of electricity that is a measure of the amount of current flowing through a conductor. *See also* ohm, volt.

**amplifier:** A device that increases the power, number of volts, or number of amperes of an electric current. *See also* ampere, volt.

**amplitude:** The greatest amount that a wave rises above or dips below a middle value.

**anode:** A positive electrode; the electrode to which electrons move in electric and electronic devices. *See also* electrode.

**atom:** One of the extremely small particles of which all matter is made. *See also* electron, molecule, proton.

**audio frequency:** In radio, the frequency of the electrical waves generated by sound entering a microphone. *See also* frequency.

**bimetallic strip:** A strip made up of two metal strips fastened together along their entire lengths. This strip bends when its temperature is changed.

**calibrate:** To make measuring marks on an object.

**carrier frequency, or carrier wave:** In radio and television, electromagnetic waves that have equal and unvarying wavelengths and amplitudes. *See also* frequency.

**cathode:** A negative electrode; the electrode from which electrons move in electric and electronic devices. *See also* electrode.

**cell:** *See* electric cell.

**ceramic:** Made of clay.

**charge:** Any given amount of electricity in or on an object.

**coil:** In electricity, a number of turns of wire, usually in spiral form.

**combustion:** A chemical change which produces light and heat; burning.

**conduction:** The transfer of heat from molecule to molecule of a substance. The transfer of free electrons from atom to atom of a substance. *See also* conductor, free electron, molecule.

**conductor:** A substance that offers relatively little resistance to the transfer of heat or electrons.

**convection:** Transfer of heat by circulation currents in gases and liquids.

**cycle:** In radio, television, and electricity, one complete wavelength.

**d.c.:** *See* direct current.

**direct current:** Electric current that flows continuously in only one direction. Abbreviated d.c. or D.C.

**dry cell:** An electric cell whose contents are moist, and sealed so they will not spill.

**element:** A substance which has not been resolved into simpler substances by chemical means.

**electric cell:** A device for producing electric current by chemical means.

**electricity:** The movement and other actions of electrons in conductors.

**electrode:** An anode or a cathode. *See also* anode, cathode.

**electromagnet:** An iron rod or core surrounded by a coil of insulated wire through which passes an electric current in order to produce a temporary magnet.

**electromagnetic waves:** Waves of energy produced by movements of electric charges in a magnetic field. These include radio, television, electric, and light waves.

**electron:** A unit charge of negative electricity. One of the negatively charged particles that make up the outer structure of an atom.

**electronics:** The study and use of the movement of electrons in electron tubes, transistors, and diodes. Unlike electricity, electronics does not deal with the movement of electrons through conductors.

**e.m.f.:** Electromotive force. *See also* volt.

**energy:** The ability to do work. Energy has many forms: heat, light, electrical, mechanical, chemical, and others.

**evaporation:** The change of a liquid to a gas. This change takes place with or without raising the temperature of the liquid above its surroundings.

**Fahrenheit:** A temperature scale in which the freezing point is at 32° and the boiling point is at 212° . The scale was named for its inventor, Daniel Gabriel Fahrenheit (1686-1736), a German physicist.

**field:** In electricity, the space in which an electric current can be detected. In magnetism, the space in which magnetic force can be detected surrounding a magnet or a moving electric charge.

**filament:** In electricity and electronics, a thin wire or coil of wire made of metal with high electrical resistance so that it becomes incandescent (red-hot or white-hot) when electric current is sent through it. The incandescent filament is used as a source of heat, light, or electrons.

**fluorescence:** The property of substances that absorb radiation of shorter wavelengths and, as a result, emit radiation of longer wavelengths as long as the shorter radiation is being absorbed. Also, fluorescence is the emitted radiation.

**FM:** A system of radio broadcasting in which the frequency of a carrier wave is varied, or modulated by an audio frequency current. FM stands for *frequency modulation. See also* AM, audio frequency.

**force:** A push or pull that produces or destroys motion, increases or lessens the rate of motion, changes the direction of motion, or changes the shape of a body.

**frequency:** The number of complete wavelengths that occur in a unit of time, usually one second.

**hertz:** A unit of frequency equal to one cycle per second.

**insulator:** A material that offers great resistance to the transfer of heat or electric current.

**Law of Electric Charges:** Like charges repel; unlike charges attract.

**Law of Magnetic Poles:** Like poles repel; unlike poles attract.

**mechanism:** Any machine or part of a machine; any operation or action of a machine.

**molecule:** The smallest particle of a substance that keeps the characteristics of the substance when undergoing chemical change.

**momentum:** A measure of the amount of force needed to bring a moving body to rest.

**ohm:** A unit of electricity that is a measure of the resistance of a conductor to the flow of electric current. *See also* ampere, conductor, volt.

**oscillator:** An electron tube or other device for producing alternating current, specifically, radio frequency current for use as a carrier frequency, or carrier wave. *See also* alternating current, carrier frequency.

**photoelectric cell:** An electron tube that generates electric current when exposed to light.

**proton:** A positively charged particle in the nucleus of an atom; a unit charge of electricity.

**radio frequency:** An alternating current that is used in radio broadcasting to produce the carrier wave; the carrier frequency. *See also* alternating current, carrier frequency.

**rectifier:** An electron tube or other device used to change alternating current to direct current. *See also* alternating current, direct current.

**resistance:** Opposition to electric current offered by a conductor. *See also* conductor, ohm.

**semiconductor:** A solid whose ability to conduct electric current is between that of a conductor and an insulator. *See also* conductor, insulator.

**siphon:** A device consisting of a tube in the shape of an upside-down "U," which, due to atmospheric pressure, can be used to cause liquids to flow over barriers.

**stator:** Stationary blades in a steam turbine. Stationary part of an electric generator.

**switch:** In electricity, a device for starting and stopping the flow of electricity; a device for making and breaking an electric circuit.

**thermostat:** Device for regulating temperature, using a bimetallic strip. *See also* bimetallic strip.

**triode:** An electron tube containing an emitter, plate, and grid.

**ultraviolet:** Electromagnetic radiation having a wavelength slightly shorter than that of violet light.

**vapor:** A substance in the gaseous state, as distinct from the solid or liquid state.

**volt:** A unit of electricity that is a measure of the electromotive force (e.m.f.) needed to drive one ampere of current through one ohm of resistance. *See also* ampere, ohm.

**watt:** A unit of power, electrical or mechanical.

# INDEX

144

146